Marko Pogačnik
Grimm's Fairy Tales Decoded
Precious messages
from the past for the future

This book was first published
in German by Neue Erde (2024)

© Marko Pogačnik, 2025
illustrations © Marko Pogačnik, 2024

Translation © Tadej Turnšek and Rahel Ries

The right of Marko Pogačnik, to be identified
as the author of this work has been asserted
in accordance with the Copyright, Designs
and Patents Act, 1988

First published in 2024 by Istros Books
London, United Kingdom
www.istrosbooks.com

Edited by Susan D. Curtis

Design and layout: pikavejica.com

Printed by CMP, Poole, Dorset, UK

ISBN: 978-1-912545-50-6

The publishers wish to thank the VITAAA
Association for Coexistence of Humanity,
Nature, and Space from Ljubljana, Slovenia,
for generously financing the translation from
Slovenian into English, and the Arts Council
England for their support of the work of
Istros Books.

Marko Pogačnik

Grimm's Fairy Tales Decoded

Precious messages
from the past for the future

Translated from the Slovenian by
Tadej Turnšek

The Story of the Fisherman and his Wife
and One-eye, Two-eyes and Three-eyes
translated from German stories by
Rahel Ries

mimosa

Contents

- 7   Foreword
- 9   Preface
- 13   The Frog King or Iron Henry
- 23   Sleeping Beauty
- 34   Snow White
- 50   Little Red Riding Hood
- 58   The Wolf and the Seven Little Goats
- 66   Cinderella
- 82   Rumpelstiltskin
- 90   Hansel and Gretel
- 99   The Star Money
- 103   Rapunzel
- 115   The Devil With the Three Golden Hairs
- 126   The Story of the Fisherman and His Wife
- 138   One-eye, Two-eyes and Three-eyes

Foreword

Susan D. Curtis

Marko Pogačnik is a very special person: an artist since the early 1960's, a sculptor, a writer and ecologist, as well as a social activist. He is a supremely creative human being who incorporates the creative potential of art into diverse life processes. A member of the Slovenian OHO art collective movement, a founder of the Šempas Family, an agricultural and artistic commune that also functioned as a spiritual centre, he currently works in stone, installing carved standing stones at energetic points worldwide, a process of earth healing he calls 'Lithopuncture'.

An older sculpture of rambling wooden beams, some of them defunct railway sleepers, was the scene of our most recent meeting. Leading me along the undulating rampways, he explained that the rhythm of the piece echoes the cyclic year; from equinoxes to solstices. At the juncture of one curve, a self-seeded tree had grown tall in the thirty-odd years since he first made the piece, spreading its leaves in a welcome canopy to protect us from the strong sun that day, and seeming like nature's approving response to Marko's artistic gesture.

Such outdoor sculptures bring Marko into an intimate dialogue with nature, and like all those who work with Mother (Sister) Earth, he feels her on many emotional levels. It was not that long ago that all of us lived close to the land and had the time – and the silence – to witness the natural processes and the more subtle realms of worldly phenomena. Not that long ago, too, when fairies and elves and spirits of the woods were our companions as much as dogs and cats, for people have always lived through the imagination alongside the physical experience. Spirituality is as much part of our nature as is creativity, and Marko's interpretations of these beloved tales bring us back to their deeper meanings, remind us that beyond our everyday rational experience there is the steady causal background, the world of ideas and metaphysical truths which give us symbols and archetypes. Embodied in the human and animal characters of these stories are truths about our own natures and the nature of the realm we reside in, yet have become estranged from; lessons in how to live in harmony with the elemental forces and our fellow creatures.

I encourage you to open your minds and hearts and let Marko lead you, too, through his words and pictures...

Preface

In order to invite you to listen to my retelling of Grimm's Fairy Tales, I must first point out that 'fairy tales' were not originally intended for children. Nor were they invented by the brothers Wilhelm and Jakob Grimm at the turn of the 19th century, during the Romantic period. The brothers Grimm actually drew on folk tradition to write down the stories, which means that they had been passed from storyteller to storyteller for centuries before that, intended for adults on winter evenings, when the farming work was done and the livestock tended, and people were eager to learn about the secrets of living on this Earth. The Bible and religious sermons were unable to satisfy this desire, since they were primarily concerned with the projection of eternity onto earthly soil, consciously glossing over the dimensions of earthly spirituality. The folk traditions, on the other hand, are mostly concerned with the wisdom of the Earth and its vital worlds.

This precious indigenous tradition would not have survived the narrowmindedness of the 19th century if it were not for the Grimm brothers, who rewrote it into fairy tales for children. Thus, it survived safely stored in children's rooms for the next two centuries, when the rational view of life had almost completely suppressed the mystery of existence between Heaven and Earth. I am convinced that human consciousness is now mature enough to look beyond the juvenile disguise and listen to the cosmic archetypes hidden in *Snow White*, *Sleeping Beauty*, *Cinderella* and other tales of ancient times preserved for us by the Grimm brothers.

It makes sense to dedicate a book to them in 2024, as the many translations into different languages over the last hundred years and more have helped to firmly root Grimm's fairy tales in the emotional world and memories of countless generations of children. But these children have not remained children, they have grown up. Although they may not remember *The Frog King or Iron Henry*, they carry in their subconscious a record of the existence of the elemental beings of nature, and with it the key to becoming aware of their true existence and their role in the universe of life, nature and humanity.

If you allow me, I will try to activate this key within you. My way of telling Grimm's Fairy Tales is to translate the faery language of the story into terms that a modern person can understand, enabling them to integrate the message into their way of looking at the world and life. In doing so, I rely on my experience in healing the degraded spaces of nature and human culture, which I have been doing for decades. While working with the vital and spiritual worlds of the Earth and the landscape, I have noticed a kinship with certain archetypes embodied in Grimm's fairy tales. I know them because I used to read them to my daughters. Later, in the early 1990s, when I was writing my book on Elemental Beings and Nature Spirits, I was surprised to find that almost every encounter with them was a fairy tale in itself, and I began to talk publicly about my 'fairy tale' experiences. As a storyteller, I always included some of the stories of the Grimm brothers, until my own retellings of the Grimm myths had accumulated into a whole book – which is now before you.

I would also like to remind you that the Grimm brothers adapted the stories to their own rational ideas of what children can grasp and what they need to be protected from. I therefore believe that many of their formulations do not correspond to the original tales, but are deliberately reduced to the level of the supposed horizon of children's imagination – which is in fact the belief horizon of that period, where it was assumed that children were immature beings and not (yet) capable of grasping the truth of life. Fortunately, I am able to look into the causal backgrounds of the texts at certain points, and in some places I have reconstructed the original course of the story in order to make sense of its message.

I will begin with *The Frog King*, the first of Grimm's fairy tales that opened up to me after I had made direct contact with the elemental beings of nature.

The Frog King or Iron Henry

Close by the king's castle lay a great dark forest. In the middle of the forest was a very old and very deep well, where the king's youngest daughter would go when the day was particularly warm. She sat down by the side of the well, and when she was bored, she took a golden ball in her hand, and threw it up in the air.

But on one occasion, the princess's golden ball did not fall back into her outstretched hands, but past them into the darkness of the deep well, and lay in the mud at the bottom. The king's daughter followed it with her eyes, but the well was so deep that the bottom could not be seen. At this she began to cry, and cried louder and louder, and could not be comforted. And as she thus lamented, she heard a strange voice: "What ails you so, daughter of the king? Your weeping would even move a stone to pity."

The opening passage of the story brilliantly describes the distress in which the soul essence of a human being finds itself during its embodiment in matter. The king's daughter, white-skinned and wearing silken veils, represents a human being existing in the spaces of eternity before it decides to descend the path of embodiment towards the density of matter. The golden ball which the princess throws towards the sky is a sign of perfection and speaks of the state which the soul enjoys in the primeval space of eternity before embarking on the path of embodiment. The sphere is the most perfect of all forms, and gold the most precious of all minerals.

The fall of the sphere into a deep, dark, narrow well is symbolic of the landing of the soul in the earthly space, severely limited by the density of matter, equal to the experience of the soul after birth. The weeping and wailing of the princess point to the mental distress that a human being experiences, not only after birth itself, but often and repeatedly during the period of our embodiment. We yearn for the light, the freedom and the infinity of the etheric spaces where the soul essence of a human being dwells in the period between two embodiments.

When the princess looks around to see where the strange voice is coming from, she sees a frog and says: "Ah, old water-splasher, I am weeping for my golden ball, which has fallen into the well." The frog comforts her and assures her that he is able to retrieve the ball from the mud in which it is stuck, adding, "But what will you give me if I pick up the golden ball from the well?"

I equate the encounter between the beautiful princess and the 'ugly' frog with the encounter between the soul essence of a human being and a being from the elemental world of Earth. This kind of encounter after birth is unavoidable, because we equate elemental beings with the natural forces and consciousness that enables life to exist and evolve in the conditions of matter. If we, as a human race, have chosen to accelerate our evolution through the experiences we accumulate during our various incarnations, we cannot avoid the help of the elemental world. It is no coincidence that the crouching frog is chosen as a symbol of the elemental being. His body clings to the Earth and has completely different proportions from the human body. The frog perfectly represents a being of the Earth. However, the fairy tale does not equate the frog only with nature because it gives him the ability to speak and empathise. This means

During the process of embodiment,
the ball of soul perfection
falls into a deep well.

that elemental beings are not one of the evolutions embodied in matter, as is the case with plants, rocks and animals. The elemental beings represent consciousness and creative acts operating in the causal background of the embodied world. However, since the frog requires something in return for his help, we can think of elemental beings as primarily beings of consciousness, involved in the cycles of regulating and transforming the life currents, and as such accountable for their work to their originator, Sister Earth.

The princess is so eager to regain the perfection she experienced as an unborn soul that she is willing to give the frog all her wealth in exchange: "I give you my fine clothes, my pearls and jewels, and even the golden crown which I am wearing." But the frog says to her: "I do not care for your clothes, your pearls and jewels, nor for your golden crown, but if you will love me and let me be your companion and play-fellow, and if I may sit by your side at your little table, and eat off your little golden plate, and drink out of your tiny cup, and sleep in your little bed – if you will promise me all this I will go down below, and bring you your golden ball back again." Of course, she promised the frog all it wanted, only to get her golden ball back, while she thought to herself, "How the silly frog does talk. All he does is to sit in the water with the other frogs, and croak. He can be no companion to any human being."

The passage is remarkably clear in offering the key to the cooperation between people and the elemental world of Earth and nature. It argues that the elemental consciousness of nature and its life forces are not merely a phenomenon of our environment – as rational consciousness, armed with the countless findings of science, would have us believe – they are part of us and we, as embodied beings, are part of them. That is why the frog refuses the offered goods and transfers the relationship between people and the elemental world into the human interior. It straightforwardly conveys the message that it is only with the help of the elemental beings that a human being is capable of surviving in the embodied world and also of performing creative acts.

At that moment, a leap to another level occurs. The frog is no longer just a symbol of the elemental consciousness of nature, but reveals itself as a personal elemental being. Just as the different kinds of elemental beings take care of trees, plant life, stones, water circulation and so on, the personal elemental being takes care of all the conditions necessary for the individual human being to be able to spend the period of his embodiment from birth to death in a healthy, creative and contented way.

The Frog precisely defines the areas where the elemental being enables the three fundamental values of life to be enjoyed by the human being:

- "Eating from the same plate and drinking from the same glass" refers to the valuable role of the personal elemental being in managing and balancing the organic processes in the human body.
- I understand "playing together" – to take the expression out of the context of a fairy tale intended for children – as participation in creative processes. It is elementary consciousness that enables the human being to translate his ideas and actions into material forms.
- "Sleeping in the same bed" means the continuous coexistence of the human soul and the elemental being in the same body, from human conception to the completion of the processes after death.

The following day, when the princess sits at the table with the king and the courtiers, eating from her golden plate, there is a knock at the door and a voice cries: "Princess, youngest princess, open the door for me!" The princess runs to see who is knocking, but when she opens the door and sees a frog sitting in front of it, she slams the door and returns to the table. The king notices her agitation and, when he hears what she has promised the frog, he demands that she keep her promise. She has to let the frog into the dining room and lift him up on the table, and the frog says: "Push your little golden plate nearer to me that we may eat together."

At this point, we have come across a traumatic pattern that is characteristic of a modern human being, driving him into a state of alienation from nature, the Earth, and himself. The rational consciousness developed over the last two or three millennia does not allow for the idea that human beings could cooperate with the beings of nature. It sees nature as the environment that surrounds civilisation and the life processes within a human being as a kind of organic automatism. We are no longer fond of the idea that life is created in the cooperation, mutual conversation and companionship of two different kinds of consciousness and beings, which complement each other and cooperate based on mutual trust and love, even though they are essentially different.

Of course, the coexistence of human and elemental beings does not exist on the material level. In order to be able to let it into our consciousness and into our emotional world, we have to be aware that the cooperation takes place on a subtle level, where the levels of the human soul and the elemental world meet. The fairy tale translates the collaboration between the two onto the level of embodiment, so that the listeners can grasp how fatally dangerous for modern humans and for our health is this resistance we feel upon contact with the elemental consciousness, especially when it occurs within ourselves.

The disgust and aversion towards a being of a different kind – even though it allows us to live in the embodied world – reaches its peak when the frog wants to lie down with the princess in her bed. The princess is so angry that she throws the frog against the wall, saying, "Now, will you be quiet, odious frog!" At that moment, a miraculous transformation takes place. The

The frog said, "Lift me up on the table, we'll eat together."

frog is transformed into a prince with kind and beautiful eyes. Immediately, the princess falls in love with him and wants to marry him.

Thanks to physics, there is a modern term for this miraculous transformation, a 'quantum leap'. Death that occurs on one level allows for a leap and rebirth on the next, higher level of existence. With the disappearance of the frog, its higher level of being could be revealed, and this is equal in value to that of the princess. The elemental essence of the beings of nature can be equated with royal dignity, comparable to the soul essence of a human being. Such recognition of the spiritual equivalence of two beings belonging to two different branches of evolution leads to coexistence in peace and love. The fairy tale marks this happy mutual recognition with a wedding celebration.

After the human and the elemental being have realised that they complement each other and love each other, the prince invites the princess to marry him in his kingdom. A coachman named Henry comfortably seats the wedding couple in the carriage, while he himself stands on the step behind the carriage, takes the reins and commands the eight white horses to start the journey.

Well on their way, the prince hears a loud cracking noise behind him as if something had broken. He turns round and cries, "Henry, the carriage is breaking!" But Henry replies: "No, master, it is not the carriage. It is a band from my heart that's broken!"

They are back on their way, when the prince hears a loud bang behind his back again, as if something had broken. He turns to Henry and cries, "Henry, the carriage is breaking!" "No, master, it is not the carriage. It's just the second band from my heart that's broken!"

Once again on their way, the prince hears a loud bang behind his back again, as if something had broken. He turns to Henry and cries, "Henry, the carriage is breaking!" "No, master,

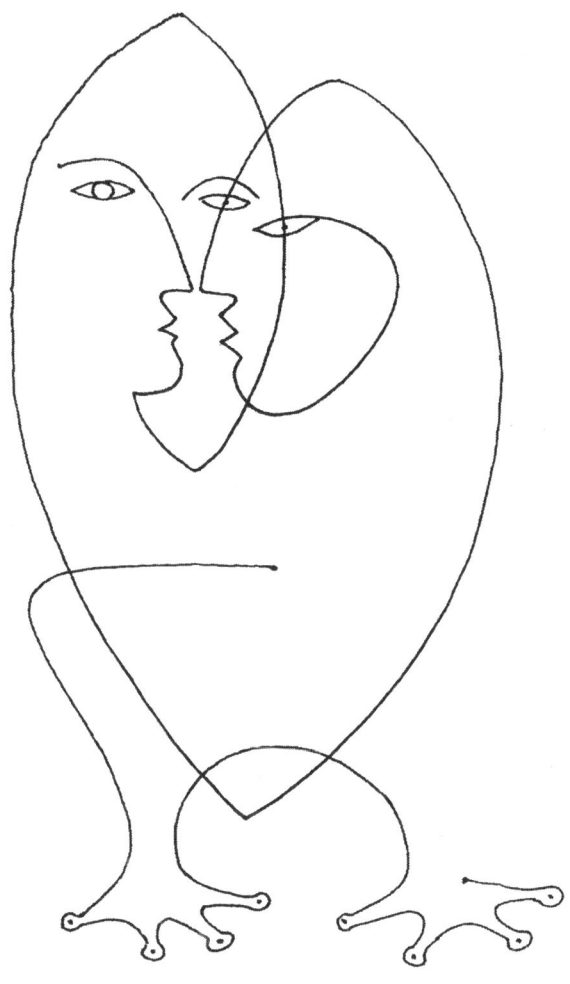

Happiness comes when one
recognises an elemental
being as one's equal.

it is not the carriage. It's just the third band from my heart that's broken!"

In the first years of my retelling of the Frog King, I ignored the part of the tale with Iron Henry as unnecessary. The relationship changed instantly when I conducted a landscape workshop on the island of Gotland in the middle of the Baltic Sea in August 2014. As we explored the ruins of the once mighty Buttle Änge Monastery, I came across a host of small elemental beings. I felt that they were trying to tell me something as a member of the human race, but I did not understand them. They insisted, and finally the story of Iron Henry with three cruel bands on his heart was brought back to my mind. I finally understood that they wanted to draw my attention to the three main blockages that prevent genuine contact between the human race and the beings of the Earth and Nature – the elemental beings. This is how the 'frogs' of Gotland translated the three iron bands on the human heart into the language of my consciousness:

- Human beings deny being part of nature and the elemental worlds of the Earth. We have closed ourselves off in our exclusively human world.
- Human beings enslave other embodied beings of the Earth, as if plants, animals and minerals were not beings in their own right with their own consciousness and purpose of existence.
- Human beings lock the beings of parallel worlds, both visible and invisible, into the narrowness of their own mental patterns, preventing us all from being free to exist as who we really are. Furthermore, only the materialized beings of nature are allowed to show themselves in the daylight. All other more subtle extensions of nature must stay concealed behind the curtain of the manifested world.

Sleeping Beauty

For centuries, mankind has been plagued by the question of how it is possible that we have found ourselves in an age of increasing alienation, both from each other and from the beings of the Earth and the elemental beings of nature. Sleeping Beauty provides the answer, hidden in the language of fairy tales.

Once upon a time there lived a king and a queen, both of whom wanted a child very much. And it so happened that one day the queen went for a swim in a nearby pond. As she was coming out of the water, a frog appeared on a leaf of a bay tree and said: "Your wish shall be fulfilled, and before a year passes you will bring a daughter into the world."

I would like to point out that ancient narratives often take place within royal families, but this should not be attributed to medieval influences alone. In fairy-tale language, the queen and the king denote a more complete (or 'higher') level of human being, i.e. the level of human eternal soul. Together with princes and princesses, they address the so-called causal dimension of the world, which exists beyond space and time. There, the patterns of all that exists pulsate. They are the origin of all that we know in the embodied world of nature and culture. By contrast, the farmer, the miller or the craftsman mark the embodied level of everyday life.

We already know the frog as a symbol of the elemental (invisible, causal) world of nature from The Frog King. And so, the story of Sleeping Beauty tells us quite straightforwardly at the very beginning that conception is not possible without the participation of an elemental being. No matter how much the King and Queen want a child, Sleeping Beauty's soul cannot be incarnated without the touch of a frog or the cooperation of the elemental world of Earth, because the latter is responsible for the processes of incarnation.

Indeed, it happened as the frog predicted, and the Queen gave birth to a baby girl. The girl was so beautiful that the king could not contain himself for joy, and he ordered a great celebration. But he invited not only relatives and acquaintances, but also the wise women – the Fates, so that they would be kindly disposed toward the child. There were thirteen of them in his kingdom, but because he had only twelve golden plates from which they were to eat, one of them had to remain at home.

When the feast was over, the wise women came to the cradle and presented the girl with their magic gifts: The first gave her virtue, the second one beauty, the third one wealth, and so on with everything that one could wish for on Earth.

Do not believe that the king didn't have the 13th golden plate! The rejection of the thirteenth Fate represents an important key that unlocks the mystery of that era in human evolution that still plagues us today. I am referring to the era marked by the rather rigid domination of the masculine principle and male forces. Twelve is the number of the solar year with its twelve months, and thirteen is the symbol of the year following the phases of the lunar transformation, known to older cultures and based on the principle of Goddess.

There are actually thirteen months. However, patriarchal cultures have wanted to split the 13th month and divide it among the other 12, thus suppressing it and hiding it from our eyes, just as the king ignored the existence of the thirteenth Fate.

Contact with an elemental
being enabled the Queen to
give birth to a baby girl.

Why is the suppression of the thirteenth Fate, and thus of the feminine principle, so important that it diverted the course of the princess's life? The masculine principle is focused on the profits of constant growth, it desires eternal peace and worships goodness. These are indeed positive virtues in themselves, but they become a cause for violence because – in the absence of cyclical principle – they have to be enforced by force. In patriarchal cultures, the quest for perpetual peace turns into perpetual wars – just look at the world around you!

The feminine principle does not have to enforce these same values. It relies on an eternal flow of transformation and renewal of life. Just as the moon's phases alternate in a circle between darkness and light, life flows between birth, death and rebirth. If the thirteenth Fate, who represents the wheel of transformation, is absent, life within the male-dominated (patriarchal) will to power weakens and gradually dies, as we are experiencing today in the context of so-called climate change.

Just as the eleven wise women had made their predictions about the child's future, the thirteenth Fate unexpectedly arrived on the scene and announced: "In the princess's fifteenth year she shall prick herself with a spindle and fall over dead." And without saying another word she turned around and left.

Then the twelfth wise woman, who had not yet offered her wish, stepped forward. As she was unable to refute the grave prediction, but only to soften it, she said, "However, this will not be the final death. The princess will only fall into a hundred-year deep sleep."

In order to rescue his beloved daughter from the predicted faith, the king issued an order that all spinning wheels, including spindles, in the entire kingdom should be burned. And the girl grew as beautiful, virtuous, friendly and intelligent as the wise women had predicted.

Here, the fairy tale reminds the human race that the suppression of the feminine principle and the absolute preference for

After the eleven wise women had given their gifts to the princess, the thirteenth Fate suddenly walked in.

the masculine way of treating life and the world inevitably backfires. Good intentions dedicated to the progress and well-being of people and humanity can quickly turn into their opposite. Fortunately, here comes the twelfth Fate as a symbol of divine grace. She carries the message that the human imperfections or misconceptions that cause us to fall from one misfortune to another are not fatal after all. We human beings enjoy the gift of life above all to learn, and with it to find out what is true and what is alien or even contrary to the truth. Even unfortunate experiences, if we internalise them, are important for our development. We should not be punished for them more than is necessary to make us realise the errors in our thinking or actions.

As it happened, on the day when the princess turned fifteen years of age, the king and the queen were not at home, and the little girl was left all alone in the castle. She wandered around, looking at the rooms and chambers as her heart desired. Finally, she came to an old tower. She climbed up the narrow, winding stairs and arrived at a small door. There was a rusty key in the lock, and when she turned it, the door sprang open. There in a small room sat an old, wrinkled woman with a spindle, busily spinning wool.

"Good day, grandma," the princess greets her. "What are you doing here?" "I am spinning," said the old woman, nodding her head kindly. "What is that thing that is so merrily bouncing about?" asked the girl, taking hold of the spindle. And as soon as she touched the spindle, the magic curse was fulfilled and the princess pricked herself on her finger. The next moment she fell onto a nearby bed and slipped into a deep sleep.

It is no coincidence that the tragic event took place in an abandoned and forgotten tower and in the room of a woman as old as the Earth. We are dealing with the memory of ancient cultures that respected and lived the cyclical principle of life, as manifested, for example, in the changing of the seasons or in the phases in the intimate part of a woman's body. The room in the old tower and Grandmother Earth behind the spinning wheel represent a living memory of the life values that were gradually discarded by a human race that increasingly relied on the power of rational thought.

It is also no coincidence that the princess pricked her finger on the spinning wheel, a symbol of the rhythmic-cyclical creation of the thread of life. In spinning, a tangled pile of wool – a symbol of primordial chaos – is transformed into a beautifully ordered thread suitable for weaving the fabric of life.

Nor it is coincidence that that the princess pricked her finger with a tiny piece of the spinning wheel called a spindle. It looks like a piece of wood shaped like a letter U, pierced in the middle by a metal needle representing the axis around which the reel rotates while the spun thread is wound around it. This is the only part of the spinning wheel that the princess could prick herself with. I associate the spindle with a special 'wheel' in human consciousness called the faculty of rational thought. Although this 'wheel' represents only a small part of our ability to think comprehensively, in the era of the domination of masculine principle, in the so-called patriarchal age, it has become the leading and exclusive way of looking at the world. Continuing from this point on, the fairy tale talks about the consequences of subjection to the powers of the rational mind.

The princess's sleep instantly spread throughout the entire castle. The king and queen, who had just returned home, fell asleep, and all of their attendants as well. The horses fell asleep in their stalls, the dogs in the courtyard, the pigeons on the roof, the flies on the walls, and even the fire on the hearth flickered, stopped moving, and fell asleep. The cook, who was about to pull the kitchen boy's hair for having done something wrong, went numb in the middle of it and fell asleep. The wind stopped blowing, and outside the castle not a leaf was stirring in the trees.

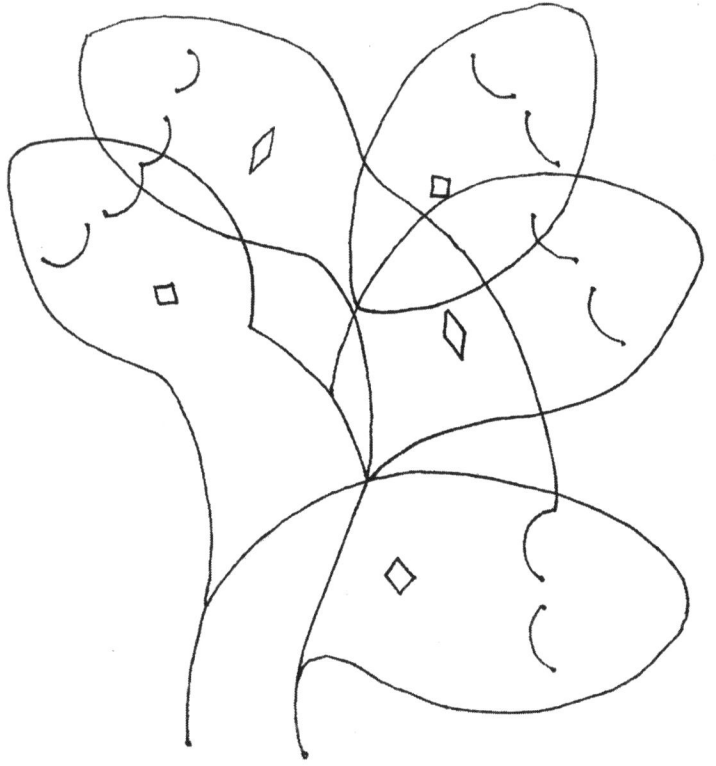

The princess's sleep instantly spread throughout the entire castle.

The passage clearly confirms that the way people look at life around them and the way they see themselves has a decisive influence on the state of the world. Like Sleeping Beauty, the human being has fallen asleep in the narrowness of his intellect. But he has not kept his sleep to himself: the narrowness of his intellect, which is not aware of the subtle regions of existence invisible to the organic eye, has also infected nature and his entire environment with it. Is this even possible? Doesn't the fairy tale say that the dogs in the yard and the flies on the wall fell asleep together with the princess (who represents the human race)?

People are incredibly powerful creative beings. If we convince ourselves – as was the case during the last millennia of our evolution – that there is nothing that the eyes cannot see or the hands cannot touch, then this conviction is transferred as a pattern to the circumstances of life in which we live. Over the last two centuries, scientific disciplines have produced mountains of evidence that this is the case. The more convincing the evidence (which is also conceived by human beings), the more humanity believes in its own image of the world. As a consequence, all of nature, along with countless creatures, is forced to sink into a slumber of narrowed consciousness. The story of Sleeping Beauty is able to paint the situation in which humanity has found itself, and with it the worlds of nature, in a brilliant, sensually illustrative way.

Around the castle a thorn hedge began to grow, and every year it became higher, until it finally surrounded and covered the entire castle and extended beyond it, so that even the flag at the top of the tallest tower could no longer be seen.

From time to time, princes and knights came and tried to force their way through the hedge into the castle, but sadly ended up stuck in the thorns. But a hundred years to the day after the princess pricked herself so unfortunately, a young man came to the country who was not afraid of thorns and was determined to get through to the princess.

But behold, as the prince approaches the thorn hedge, it was nothing but large, beautiful roses that separated themselves and allowed him to pass through to reach the Sleeping Beauty. She lay before him so beautiful that the prince could not take his eyes off her lips. He bent over and gave her a kiss, thereby waking her up.

At that moment, the king awoke, and the queen, and all the royal attendants. The horses in the courtyard stood up and shook themselves. The hunting dogs jumped and wagged their tails. The pigeons on the roof pulled their little heads out from beneath their wings and flew into the field. The flies on the walls crept about again, and the fire in the kitchen broke into flames. The cook boxed the boy's ears and the maid continued to prepare lunch.

The last scene of The Sleeping Beauty says the most about why the tale was conceived and why people have loved to pass it orally from generation to generation. It assured them, as it assures us today, that the misfortune of the patriarchal age does not hold the ticket to eternity. We will not have to suffer forever from arrogant rulers, nor from the unjust social order that creates the rich and leaves others in poverty, nor from strongmen armed to the teeth.

The symbolic hundred years mean that we are the sufferers of an age with a limited duration. The wheels of the cosmic cycle have deposited it on Earth to give us humans and all the other beings of the Earth a very specific, often unpleasant but necessary experience, and they will carry it back to the afterlife after the 'hundred years' have passed. This is the consolation of the Sleeping Beauty, and perhaps we need it now more than ever, as the pressure on the freedom of life flows is intensifying and the tight grip of the rational systems permeate almost all aspects of life.

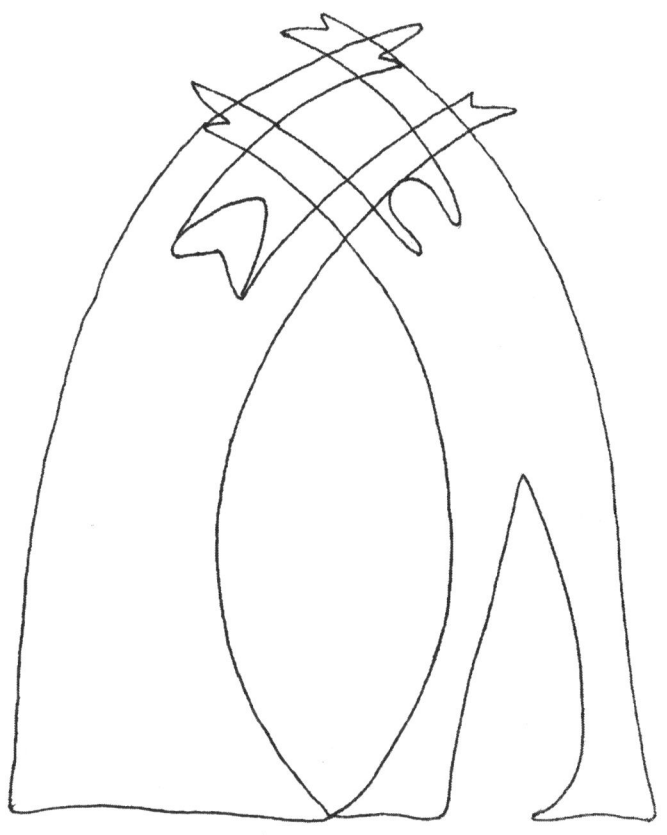

Happiness blossoms when the feminine and masculine principles are balanced and love each other.

Snow White

Snow White can shed light on the era of male domination over human society and the Earth from another angle, complementing the message of Sleeping Beauty, similarly to Cinderella.

It was the middle of winter and the snow-flakes were falling like feathers from the sky. A queen sat at her window, which was framed in black ebony, and sewed. And as she worked, gazing at times out on the snow, she pricked her finger. Three drops of red blood dripped onto the snow. And as she saw them glistening so beautifully in the white snow, the queen thought to herself: "Oh that I had a baby, white as snow, cheeks as red as blood, and hair as black as the ebony window frame."

Not very long after, the queen gave birth to a baby girl, white as snow, with cheeks as rosy as blood and hair as black as ebony. They called her Snow White.

The opening passage of the tale is marked by three colours repeated three times: white, red and black. According to the traditions of ancient cultures, the three colours repeated three times are associated with the figure of the triple Goddess, and the triple Goddess embodies the cycle of life:

- The White Goddess, also called the Virgin Goddess, embodies the principle of the interconnected whole of the Earth and the universe. She is the Goddess of Rebirth and is therefore worshipped with the blossoming of spring.
- The Red Goddess, also known as the Mother Goddess, embodies the essence of life's abundance and creativity. She is traditionally associated with high summer and the marriage between the feminine and masculine principles.
- The Black Goddess, also called Mother Death, embodies the principle of transformation that leads through death toward rebirth. She is traditionally associated with the period of late autumn and winter, when the life of nature dies only to be reborn in the spring.

The concept of the Goddess complements the concept of God, just as the feminine principle complements the masculine one. More precisely, the being of the Goddess is primordial because she embodies the movement and rotation of the cosmic cycles and cycles of life. The role of the male God is secondary. He steps in at certain points on the wheel of life, performs the function of the Goddess's partner, and then leaves again.

Snow White is testimony to an unfortunate age – one that still refuses to release its grip on us – in which masculine forces take over the role of Goddess and want to dominate life, humanity and all the beings of the Earth. The masculine forces are, of course, incapable of giving birth and of sustaining life cycles. Therefore, they appropriate feminine values through mimicry, while abandoning the love and responsibility for life that is the essence of the Goddess. On the contrary, they seize her gifts and draw them to their own will. Let's see what Snow White has to say about this perverted age:

When the baby girl was born, the queen died. A year later, the king took another wife. She was a beautiful, but haughty woman who could not bear to be surpassed in beauty. She

The archetype of the three aspects of the Goddess as virgin, mother and transformation.

had a magic mirror, and whenever she stood before it, she would ask:

"Mirror, mirror upon the wall, who is the fairest of all?"

The mirror answered: "Oh queen, you are fairest of them all."

As time passed on, Snow White grew more and more beautiful. When she was seven years old, she was more lovely than the queen herself. When the stepmother asked the mirror again one day, it told the truth: "Snow White is a thousand times more beautiful than you."

The queen was horrified and turned green with envy. Envy and pride grew in her heart like ill weeds higher every day, until she had no peace, day or night. At last, she sent for a huntsman, and ordered him, "Take this child out into the woods, I don't want to see her again. Put her to death and bring me her lungs and liver to prove it."

Historically, the destruction of the Goddess culture in Europe began in the middle of the third millennium BC with the invasion of the so-called Kurgan peoples from the Asian steppes. In the following centuries, patriarchally organised horse-riding peoples trampled on the so-called matrifocal cultures based on the cyclical principle of the Goddess and on cooperation with the elemental beings of the Earth and nature. In Europe, foreigners encountered a high culture with a rich mythical tradition, rituals and excellent skills in weaving, pottery and other handicrafts based on coexistence with nature and its beings. In the centuries that followed, newcomers – the Achaeans, the Dorians and the Ionians among the Greeks, and the Celts in different parts of Europe – took all this knowledge from the indigenous people, but imbued the traditions with their own masculine values. Out of this hybrid confusion, a new culture emerged, perfectly represented by the figure of Snow White's stepmother.

The huntsman obeyed and led the girl deep into the woods. But when he pulled out his hunting knife to pierce Snow White's heart, she began to weep and begged the hunter to let her live. "I will run away into the wild woods and never return to the castle." The huntsman was merciful and let her run away, convinced that she would be torn apart by the wild animals. He skinned a young wild boar, ripped out its lungs and liver and brought them to the queen stepmother as proof that Snow White was dead.

Snow White ran through the dark forest, barefoot over sharp stones and through thorns. Wild animals hovered around and ran past her, but did her no harm. And as the day turned to evening, she reached a wide clearing, and in the middle of it stood a small house. Dead tired, she went inside to rest.

Everything inside was very small; there was a little table covered with a white cloth, with seven little plates, each with its own little spoon, fork and knife. And by the wall were seven little beds, covered with clean white sheets. Snow White chose one of them, lay down and fell fast asleep.

The nearness of death that Snow White experienced that day and her exhausting run through the dark forest are symbols of transformation. Expelled from the rich rooms of the royal castle, she found herself barefoot among thorns and wild beasts. But such a fall does not call for our pity for the heroine. Rather, we should read it as a symbol of the transition from one dimension of existence to another. On one side of the dark forest is everyday life, governed by a patriarchal system that is not interested in values such as truth, freedom and love – or rather, these are considered second-class qualities worthy of misfits. On the other side of the dark forest, everything is different. Instead of regular plates, there are saucers on a table, along with little spoons and knives. The usual scales of things familiar from everyday life do not apply here. After passing through the dark forest, Snow White found herself in another, different world.

This other and different world is actually a mirror image of the reality we inhabit whenever we are born on Earth. We live in a manifested world, and Snow White now finds herself in what is called the causal dimension of the world. The fairy tale marks the similarity and simultaneous difference of the two worlds by the difference between a regular house and a small house, between a regular bed and a small bed, and so on. The causal dimension is one where beings exist and forces are at work that form the archetypes upon which the manifested world is formed at each moment. The tale presents the beings of the causal world as 'dwarfs'. According to the altered relations between the manifested and causal dimensions of the world, the beings of the causal dimension are no bigger than a human thumb and are therefore called dwarfs.

Late at night, the seven dwarfs returned from the mountain, where they spent the whole day searching and digging for gold. When they turned on their tiny lamps, they noticed that while they were gone, something had changed in the house.

"Who has been sitting on my chair?" said the first one.

"Who has been eating from my plate?" said the second one.

"Who has taken some of my bread?" said the third one, and so on, until they see a beautiful little girl sleeping in the bed.

When Snow White woke up the next morning, they asked her how she got into their house. She told them everything truthfully, and they invited her to stay with them to be their housekeeper, make their beds, wash their clothes, sew their clothes and keep their house neat and clean. And so, the dwarfs left early in the morning to dig for gold and returned home late at night, looking forward to a delicious dinner made by Snow White. Each morning before they left, they warned her:

"Beware of your stepmother and don't let anyone in the house."

The tale of Snow White assures humanity, suffering from the injustice of the patriarchal order: the age of the Goddess who followed the cosmic order and the cycles of nature is indeed long gone. But the daughter of the triple Goddess is still alive, although she is expelled from the embodied world and you can no

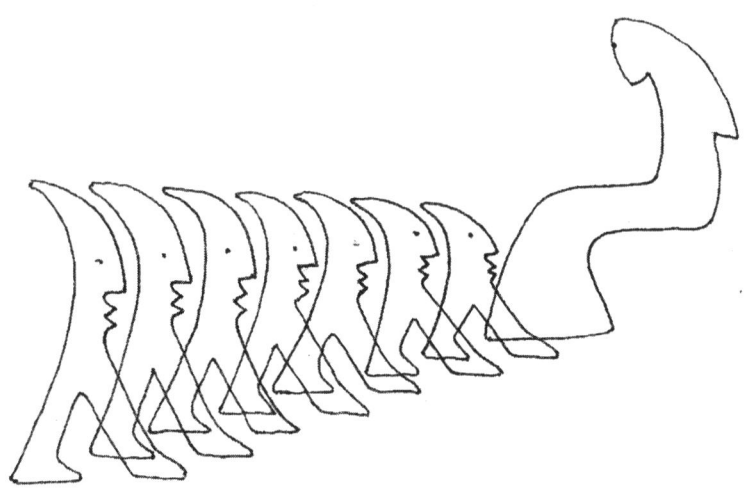

Snow White and the Seven Dwarfs.

longer enjoy her loving and righteous presence. She is currently living in the 'other world' together with the elemental beings of Earth and nature. From there, she secretly spreads her beauty and love imperceptibly among all the beings of the manifested world. If you listen deep into your hearts, you will be able to feel its blessing.

The gnomes – another term for dwarfs – were aware of the fact that the archetypes and values of the causal world spread irreversibly into the manifested world, i.e. among the beings of nature and human culture. This means that it is only a matter of time before the cruel stepmother learns that the Goddess's daughter is alive and that the outcast is taking refuge in the causal world among elemental beings. Hence their warning: "Beware of the stepmother."

Convinced that the lungs and liver she had eaten belonged to Snow White and not to the wild boar, the queen stepmother's only concern was to be first and most beautiful again. "Mirror, mirror upon the wall, who is the fairest of all?" The mirror of truth answered that although she was the most beautiful in the manifested world, Snow White, who lives with the seven dwarfs behind the seven mountains, was a thousand times more beautiful than she. So the queen stepmother hatched plans to invade the causal land of the dwarfs and get rid of her rival.

She painted her face grey and dressed herself as an old peddler so that she was unrecognisable. Thus disguised, she walked over the seven mountains to the house of the Seven Dwarfs and shouted like a peddler, "Good wares to sell — very cheap today!" Snow White peeped cautiously out of the window and asked, "Good day, good-wife, and what are your wares?" The peddler offered her a lace made of colourful silk, which Snow White liked very much. "I needn't be afraid to let this honest woman in," she thought, so she pushed open the door and bought the lace. "Come and let me lace you properly," said the peddler slyly. The unsuspecting Snow White stood up before her, but the old woman seized the opportunity and tightened the lace so tightly that it took the poor girl's breath away, and she fell to the floor as if dead.

Not long after that, the dwarfs returned from their work to find Snow White lying on the floor, seemingly dead. They hastily lifted her from the ground and cut her deadly lace. The girl began to breathe again, and slowly came back to life.

The tale describes with remarkable accuracy the problems that plague humanity after the death of the queen mother as the personification of the Goddess and the subsequent reign of a one-sided and exploitative masculine order on Earth. Snow White is not oppressed by her father, but by a depraved woman. This states loud and clear that the male principle is not in itself poisonous in nature. It only becomes toxic to humanity and threatening to the beings of nature if it is not balanced by feminine sensitivity and grace. Symbolically speaking, the God appropriates the areas of life for which the Goddess is responsible, and disaster is imminent.

The tale of Snow White goes further and reveals a carefully concealed truth. Not only does a depraved and effeminate male principal control almost all aspects of life in the manifested world – it has also discovered three different ways to secretly infiltrate the causal world and change the archetypes that guide the evolution of humanity. Snow White describes these fateful infiltrations one by one very precisely; in symbolic language, of course.

When in the story of Snow White we have the scene of being strangled by the lace, it refers to an unfortunate pattern (of behaviour) that constricts a person's waist, thus preventing the exchange between the forces of the Earth acting from below and the spiritual forces of the upper body. Humans as embodied beings can only be whole and happy when they are grounded. If they are disconnected from the Earth and nature, they lose their orientation in the embodied world and no longer know the purpose of their existence on Earth. As a result, the head becomes independent, so to speak, and allows the mind to lead it into more or less dangerous or more or less life-threatening or even life-destroying paths.

When the evil stepmother returns to the castle, she discards her disguise and rushes to the magic mirror with the same question. She feels quite sure that she is the most beautiful in the world, now that she has murdered the Goddess's daughter! But she is infuriated with the answer: "My Queen, you are the fairest here so true. But Snow White beyond the hills [expelled into the causal world] is a thousand times more beautiful than you."

"Now I will think of something that will surely be her ruin," she whispers to herself, and uses her skilled witchcraft to make a poisoned comb. Then she disguises herself as an old peddler and sets off across the seven mountains to the land of the dwarfs. She stops at their house and offers them cheap wares for sale. Snow White looks out of the window and sends her away, saying that she is forbidden to let anybody in. The pretend old woman tells her that she doesn't have to open the door, she just has to look out of the window to see what a lovely comb she has to offer. Snow White finds the shiny comb attractive and she is tempted to open the door. The peddler compliments her black hair and says: "Let me comb your hair!" But no sooner is the comb put in her hair than the poison begins to work, and the girl falls down unconscious on the floor. Fortunately, it is approaching evening and the dwarfs came home for dinner. But, horror of horrors, Snow White is lying on the ground again, as if dead. They find the poisoned comb, pull it out of her hair and Snow White comes to herself.

Of course, the appearance of a comb is associated with the head and its related concept of consciousness. But if the comb is poisonous, we are very likely dealing with certain thought patterns that have poisoned the consciousness of modern human beings. In our detailed study of Sleeping Beauty, we have already encountered the exclusionary nature of rational thought that has gripped humanity to the point of obsession in recent centuries. It excludes everything that cannot be understood and proved by logic. It excludes from modern discourse the vast areas of consciousness that pulsate beyond the wheels of reason, based on the human capacity for intuition, heart-centeredness, and imagination.

Snow White, more so than Sleeping Beauty, tells us how it was possible for a cold, rational attitude to life, to the human community and to the creatures of nature to completely capture human consciousness. It happened with the help of a poisoned comb whose many teeth faithfully reproduce the shape of a barcode. After the intrusion into the archetypes of the causal world of which Snow White speaks, humans are constantly receiving a kind of barcode as subliminal information, which states that only the rational matrix guarantees the truth and that everything else is a 'conspiracy theory'. If one is not sufficiently consciously aware, they can easily fall into the trap of the queen stepmother and begin to see their fellow free-thinkers as enemies who threaten them.

When the evil stepmother returns to the castle, she dresses herself again and rushes to the magic mirror with the same question she asked twice before. She feels quite sure that she is the most beautiful in the world, now that she has murdered the Goddess's daughter! But she is infuriated with the answer: "My Queen, you are the fairest here so true. But Snow White beyond the hills [expelled into the causal world] is a thousand times more beautiful than you."

When the stepmother heard the mirror's verdict, she rushed in anger to her secret chamber, where no one else was allowed to enter, and there she made a deadly poisoned apple. It was beautiful to look at, white on one side and red on the other, yet anyone who so much as bit into it would have died instantly. When the apple was ready, the queen painted her face again, disguised herself as a peasant woman and set off on her journey across the seven mountains to the house of the seven dwarfs.

She knocked on the door. Snow White put her head out of the window and said, "I must not let anyone in, the dwarfs have forbidden me to do so." She also refuses to take the apple that the pretend peasant woman offers her. But the latter does not take no for an answer, and to dispel Snow White's concerns that the apple might be poisoned, she bites into the white side of it herself. But the apple was so cleverly made that only the red side contained the poison, but not the white side. Convinced of the apple's harmlessness, Snow White now stretches out her hand, takes the apple from her stepmother's hand and, after taking her first bite from the red side of it, falls dead to the ground.

The queen casts on her a terrible glance, saying: "White as snow, red as blood, black as ebony! This time no dwarf can awaken you!" She rushes back home to the castle, cleans herself, dresses up in her royal attire and stands before the magic mirror with her eternal question, "Mirror, mirror upon the wall, who is the fairest of all?" This time, to her immense satisfaction, the mirror answers, "The queen, you are fairest of them all!"

The statement of the magic mirror lets us know that the third intrusion is more fatal than the other two. The first two intrusions into the causal world of the human being, while severely limiting and degrading the human essence, allow the possibility for the human being to become aware of them and to be liberated from them. According to the statement of the mirror of truth, the third intrusion seems to be definitive. As a result, the human being loses his essence and is finally lost on the earthly path – perhaps even in eternity. What could be so bad about the symbol of an apple split in two? One half is edible, the other is deadly.

We are dealing with a pattern of a fundamental split between good and the evil. In the religious sphere, such a pattern is seen in the myth of the 'Last Judgement'. At the end of time, the

Three types of patriarchal intrusion into the world of human beings and nature.

patriarchal God is supposed to divide people into two halves. The sinful and wicked go to hell, and the good and God-fearing go to heaven. The racial distinction between black and white is a recurring theme around the world. After all, this pattern of division between right and wrong is the cause of countless conflicts and wars.

Many people on Earth are aware of the dangers of the division between good and evil, and are more or less successfully avoiding it. But what do we learn from our tale if we look at the consequences of the schism through the final poisoning of Snow White? We are interested in the very thing that has us in its grip today.

What strikes the eye is the fact that the decisive poisoning of Snow White was achieved with the help of an apple. The apple is considered a symbol of a happy and fulfilled life. The poisoned apple means that the forces alien to life, embodied in the queen stepmother, have secretly cut the roots of life on Earth at the causal level. And they are doing this while explaining as loud as they can how they are trying to preserve the health of the human masses or preserve the natural environment. That would be the white half of the poisoned apple. The red half of the apple, on the other hand, appears to me as a completely parched landscape without a drop of water.

The forces acting in the name of Snow White's stepmother have cut the roots of life and, at the causal level, drained the living land to death. This is the only way they can impose their vision of the world on humanity, based on the rule of cybernetics, atomic technology, a fantastically capable internet, and robots that can provide everything people need to live their ethically and spiritually extremely impoverished lives.

The dwarfs return home in the evening to find Snow White dead. Not a breath came out of her mouth. They lay the beauty upon a bier and sit around her for three days mourning her. When the time comes to bury her, they cannot bring themselves to hide her away in the black ground. She still looks as fresh as a living person and her cheeks still glow rosy red.

So they make a special glass coffin for her so it can be looked into from all sides and placed it upon the mountain-top. And the animals come and weep for Snow White, first an owl in the name of the red Goddess, then a raven in the name of the black Goddess, and finally a dove in the name of the white Goddess. Snow White lay in her coffin for a long time and did not decay. She was still as white as snow, with her cheeks as red as blood, and her hair as black as ebony.

A faint glimmer of hope subtly shone into the tale. The archetype of the human being, and with it the freedom of the human being to grow and develop spiritually, is divine in nature. No matter how sophisticated the violence of the forces that want to subjugate it and leave it to complete alienation, it cannot completely destroy something that is of a divine nature. Snow White may be dead, but she is still alive in a way that is incomprehensible to logic. The glass coffin is a symbol of the third, cosmic space, which exists as a wide circle of divine grace beyond both the causal and the manifested world. The divine concept of the human being as a being who exists simultaneously on the spiritual and earthly level lives beyond space and time. It is a possibility that can be re-materialised at any moment.

And this is what happened. A prince from a faraway land passes by the coffin with Snow White in it and immediately falls in love with her. He begs the dwarfs to let him have her, because he loves her endlessly, even though she is dead. After much persuasion, the dwarves agree and put the coffin on their shoulders to carry it to the prince's castle. On the way, they stumble over the stump of a mighty oak tree. The shaking causes the bite of the poisoned apple to fly out of Snow White's throat. She opens her eyes, lifts the lid off her coffin, sits up and cries, "Oh dear! Where am I?"

The prince's passage from a faraway land can be understood as the orbit of a wider, cosmic cycle, capable of awakening the divine core in the human being and thus opening the way for humanity to reawaken – to awaken in the embrace of another level of time and space, hitherto unknown. Snow White's question, "Where am I?" is therefore quite appropriate.

Little Red Riding Hood

Little Red Riding Hood is a very serious tale, as it seeks to answer more precisely the question of how the dream world, or causal dimension, of the human race came to be deformed and what the consequences are of the unfortunate intrusion into it. I hope that you have already read Sleeping Beauty and Snow White, the other two heroines of the Grimm fairy tales, each of which prepares the ground for the revelation of Little Red Riding Hood from a different point of view.

Once upon a time, there was a sweet little girl whom everyone that beheld her immediately loved. But the one who loved her the most was her grandmother. One day she gave her a little red hat made of red velvet. It suited her so extremely well that she didn't want to wear anything else, so everyone called her Little Red Riding Hood.

We already know from our visit to Snow White that red is one of the three colours of the feminine aspect of divinity, and that the feminine divinity, the Goddess, embodies the cycle of life at different levels of existence. These can be the seasons of nature, the lifespan of a human being, the lunar phases, or the phases of the creative process. The colour white marks the beginning of a cycle in which everything is still integrated into a whole. The colour red is equated with the creative processes in nature and culture. The whole then blossoms, revealing the entire spectrum of life's abundance. This is followed by the wisdom of late autumn, winter and life after life as a gift from the black Goddess of Transformation.

The red colour of the red hat is an obvious reference to the creative phase of the life cycle, which is characterised by a wealth of creative processes that flow relentlessly from the causal levels into the everyday life of the manifested world. However, the fairy tale of Little Red Riding Hood puts a question mark over this flow. Is it really pure and dedicated to the music of life? What if filters have crept in between that restrict or even prevent the free flow of life's creativity?

One day, her mother sends Little Red Riding Hood to her beloved grandmother, saying, "Here in the basket is a piece of cake and a bottle of wine, take them to your grandmother. She is ill, and these goodies will make her feel better. Just walk quickly and when you get to the big forest, walk straight along the path. Don't run on the side paths, lest you fall and break the bottle."

Let us bear in mind that we are dealing with three generations, a grandmother, a mother and a daughter or granddaughter. Since the grandmother is old and sickly, she may represent a memory of an era in human development that historiography calls the younger Stone Age or Neolithic. Anthropologists speak of it as the age of the Goddess, the millennia when people followed the cycle of the triple Goddess, consciously attuning their being and life to the cycle of nature, its creatures and forces. Consequently, her granddaughter, Little Red Riding Hood, would represent the presence of the feminine principle in the present time, as well as the tragic fate that the latter is experiencing in an age of male or patriarchal domination.

The grandmother's house was in the middle of a dark forest two hours away from the village. Little Red Riding Hood sets off, and as soon as she reaches the woods, she comes across a wolf. Not knowing what a fierce beast the wolf is, she is not afraid of it, but greets it kindly: "Good morning, wolf." He answers her as if they had known each other forever: "Good morning, Little Red Riding Hood, where are you heading to so early?" "I'm going to my grandmother's house. I'm taking her a piece of cake and a bottle of wine, because she's sick and weak, so she can have a little snack and refreshment." "Little Red Riding Hood, where does your Grandma live?" "In the middle of the forest, under three tall oaks, is her little cottage, surrounded by hazel trees."

The wolf walked along with Little Red Riding Hood for a while, thinking to himself, "This will be a delicious snack; it will taste even better than the old woman; I must act wisely, and I'll eat them both."

But he said aloud to Little Red Riding Hood, "Don't you see the pretty flowers growing in the woods? Don't you hear the birds singing? Why are you in such a hurry and absorbed in thought, look around you and enjoy yourself a little!" He was going to eat Grandma first, so he wanted to distract Little Red Riding Hood and lead her away from the path.

It is no coincidence that the wolf has been chosen as a symbol for the forces that are trying to block humanity's path towards rediscovering a holistic view of the world and of its human essence. The wolf has to kill to survive. There is a good reason for this in nature, linked to the selection of species. If humans kill, it is a different matter altogether, because killing is not written in our Book of Life – the human matrix – and serves no purpose. Secondly, the wolf does not kill alone, but in packs. This is an important symbol of the forces and beings that are trying to disrupt human evolution. We are not dealing with a single huge evil creature, but with a network of life-opposing consciousness and forces working through it, which are involved at all different levels of the human world. It is no wonder, then, that the wolf knows Little Red Riding Hood by name, even though it is the first time he has met her.

The tale also perfectly illustrates the way in which these unwanted forces become involved in the life of individuals,

The modern human being is
unaware that in the causal world
he is accompanied by forces
opposed to life and truth.

communities, nations, religious associations and so on: through mimicry. They make themselves friendly and run circles around the unsuspecting souls three times before they themselves realise they have been caught in a web of counterforces.

This is what happened to Little Red Riding Hood. Following the wolf's seductive words, she suddenly noticed how the sun's rays danced through the leaves and how many beautiful flowers were all around. "If I pick a bunch of flowers, Grandma will surely be happy to have them", she thought. She ran off the path into the vast forest and started picking flowers. As she picked one, she thought she saw a more beautiful one a little further on. She ran to get it, wandering even deeper into the forest.

The wolf takes advantage of this, hurries and knocks on the door of Grandma's house. "Who's there?" asks Grandma in a weak voice. "It's me, Little Red Riding Hood," replies the wolf, "I've brought you some cake and wine, open up!" Grandma says: "Just press the handle, I'm too weak to get up and open the door for you!" The wolf presses the handle, enters, walks straight to Grandma's bed and gobbles her up. Then he puts on Grandma's nightgown and nightcap, lies down in her bed, draws the curtains and waits for Little Red Riding Hood to come so he can eat her too.

In Little Red Riding Hood, we encounter a similar symbol for the causal world as in Snow White. I am referring to Grandma's remote cottage on the other side of the vast forest, a two-hour walk from the village. Like the little house of the dwarfs it is positioned in a parallel reality. In this case, however, the village (instead of the castle) represents the everyday, so-called manifested world. It is in the causal world that the archetypes or matrixes are stored and operate upon the manifested world of everyday life, culture, technology, economics, politics and anywhere the personal experiences of the currently embodied members of the human race are being shaped at any given moment.

If the wolf has gobbled up the grandmother, who could represent the elemental consciousness of the Earth acting through the causal world, it means that there exists a force and a consciousness that is erasing the natural patterns of existence and interconnectedness and replacing them with false patterns. I am referring to patterns that direct life in the manifested world in such a way that people understand each other less and less, are less and less tolerant of each other's differences, and abandon ethical and caring values in interpersonal and international relations. The tale describes this unwelcome change by showing the wolf dressed in the grandmother's nightdress, with her nightcap on his head, lying in her bed as a substitute of her living presence.

Meanwhile, Little Red Riding Hood had picked so many flowers that she could hardly carry them. Only then did she remember her abandoned grandmother. She ran towards her cottage, and was surprised to find the door open and no one answering her greeting. With anguish in her heart, she hurried to her bed and pulled back the curtain that hid the bed from view.

Her Grandma lay before her, her nightcap pulled low over her strangely odd face.

"Oh, dear Grandma, what big ears you have!"

"All the better to hear you with, my dear."

"Oh, dear Grandma, what big eyes you have!"

"All the better to see you with."

"Oh, dear Grandma, what big hands you have!"

"All the better to grab you with."

"Oh, dear Grandma, what a big mouth you have!"

"All the better to eat you with!"

The famous dialogue between Little Red Riding Hood and the wolf explains in a hidden way how forces opposed to the development and happiness of humanity are at work. First, the eyes and ears are used as a symbol of the limited human capacity to perceive the actual reality. By manipulating the causal world,

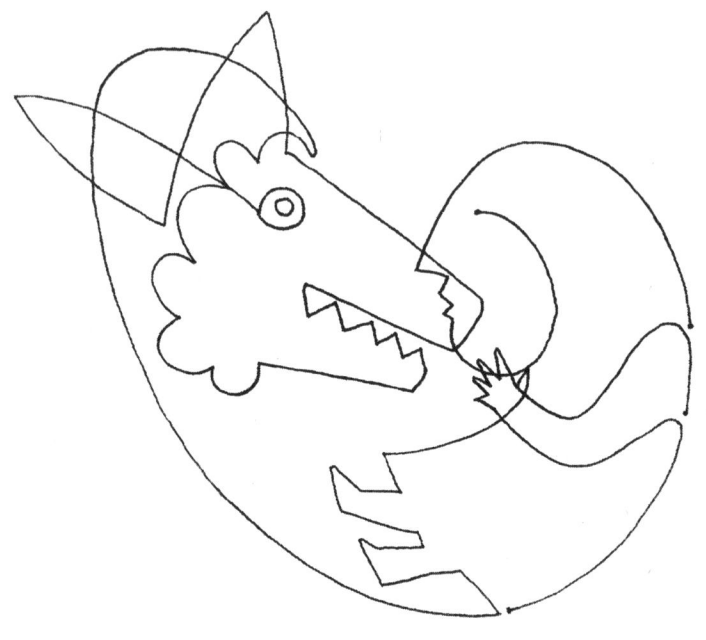

The childlike consciousness
of modern humans does not
recognise the danger it is entering
into as it walks the path of life.

they magnify our five senses to such an extent that human beings are no longer able to perceive anything beyond the material reality. We are constantly being misinformed that there is nothing beyond the material world.

Then come the hands as a symbol of action. We forget that there is a reason why we embody ourselves on Earth with our extraordinary creative capacity. We are meant to cooperate with our Mother and Sister Earth and her elemental beings in the evolution of Earth's creation. Instead, the modern human being is dominated by 'creativity' – or rather 'productiveness' – meant for his own needs or glory. People are increasingly alienated from the purpose of their existence on Earth.

When Little Red Riding Hood notices the wolf's oversized mouth, the fairy tale warns of the danger of leading people down the path of greed. An unknown force is pushing us in the direction of egocentrism and the accumulation of goods – or, at the same time, in the direction of the fear of deprivation. A person becomes a consumer of everything, provided he has the means to choose freely.

The fairy tale of Little Red Riding Hood has a happy ending, as a passing hunter shoots the wolf and rescues Grandma and Little Red Riding Hood from the wolf's belly. However, the happy ending seems contrived. We learn more about the true ending of Little Red Riding Hood in the parallel fairy tale of The Wolf and the Seven Little Goats. Let us continue with our exploration there!

The Wolf and the Seven Little Goats

Since no human person appears in the opening passage of The Wolf and the Seven Little Goats, it can be assumed that the tale is about a certain condition of life on Earth and the fate of the Earth's space. It is true, however, that the language spoken by the mother goat, her little ones and the wolf reflects the way we humans speak to each other. Therefore, we can also argue that the story is about the fate of the world as it has been decisively shaped by human culture. I am thinking of the so-called 'Anthropocene' – the age of human dominance on Earth.

Once upon a time, there was an old goat who had seven little goats. One day she had to go into the woods to fetch food for them, so she called them all round her. "Dear children," she said, "I am going out into the wood; and while I am gone, beware of the wolf. If he comes and you open the door, he will eat you all up. The wretch often disguises himself, but you will know him by his hoarse voice and black paws."

The opening part of the narrative confirms that we live in a world where different beings are at work, including those who are opposed to the flourishing of life. But there is an ancestral tradition that can help us to recognise such beings and their powers, and to ward them off. The mother goat represents the wisdom of the ancestors, capable of recognising forces alien to life and truth. They can be recognised by the way they speak, which is out of sync with the being of the whole (hoarse voice), and by the sensation that the colour of their aura evokes in a person (black paws).

Forces alien to life and truth have been perceived by ancient cultures in their ambivalent aspect, beneficial on the one hand, hostile on the other. The tale of Sleeping Beauty presents them in the form of the thirteenth, black Fate. In the case of Snow White, we are faced with the Goddess of Transformation, black as ebony. Her cosmic purpose is to break open the ever-recurring cycle of life, even to break it at a particular moment. In this way, the powers of the Goddess of Transformation create a free space in which something completely new and unusual can evolve in the celestial sphere of nature. Human culture, in turn, can use such incursions of the Black Goddess for creative acts independent of the limited space and speed of time.

Indeed, soon someone knocks on the door of the goat house, saying, "Open the door, dear children; your mother is here, and has brought something back with her for each of you." But the little goats knew that it was the wolf, by the rough voice, and do not open the door. The wolf then goes to the shopkeeper, buys a piece of chalk and swallows it to make his voice sound softer. He knocks again on the door, saying, "Open the door, dear children, your mother is here and has brought something back with her for each of you." But in doing so, the wolf unknowingly puts up his black paw against the door window, and the little goats, seeing this, knew that the wolf was at the door and did not open it.

The fairy tale first confirms the value of traditional wisdom, which helps the human being not to become a helper of the opposing forces that challenge him and try to seduce him into paths opposite to truth and love. The purpose of this challenge is to help people learn to know the difference between truth and false speech, as well as to learn to distinguish between actions that go against the flow of the cycles of life and those that support the diversity and richness of life – not only in fellow human beings, but also in oneself.

The wolf then runs to a baker and complains that he has hurt his paw and asks him to spread some dough over it. He hurries from the baker to the miller and asks him to sprinkle white flour on his paw. The miller senses that the wolf is trying to fool someone and refuses to give him the flour. The wolf then threatens to eat him up if he does not comply. The miller is afraid and spreads white flour over the wolf's paw. Thus equipped, he comes to the door for a third time and says in a soft voice: "Open the door, dear children, your mother is here, and has brought something back with her for each of you." The little kids cry out, "Show us your paw first (!) so we may know that you are really our dear mother!" The wolf puts his paw on the window and, because it is white, the little goats believe him and open the door. But, lo and behold, the wolf comes in to devour them all.

In this passage of the story, two human beings appear and with them the trace of human complicity in the destructive acts of the dark forces. The baker falls for the wolf's lies, symbolising modern man's loss of a sense of truth. The miller recognises the wolf's nefarious intentions, but is intimidated by the threat of death. Both, the fear of one's own mortality, intertwined with human indifference to the question of truth, cause the disruptive forces to leap to the level of 'higher' potency and to begin to act disruptively in the world of wholeness. Let's see how this happens.

The little goats are terrified and want to hide from the wolf's hunger. One jumps under the table, the second under the quilts on the bed, the third in the stove, the fourth in the kitchen, the fifth into the cupboard, the sixth under the sink, and the seventh into the clock case. The wolf finds six of them and devours them mercilessly. However, he did not find the youngest kid, the one who was in the clock case. After satisfying his appetite, he lies down on the grass under a lush tree and falls asleep.

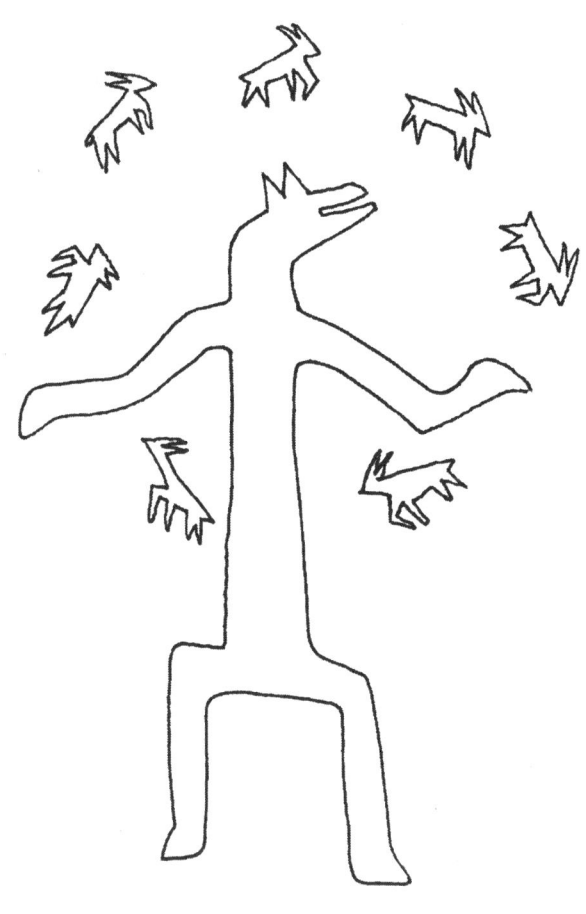

The wolf rejoices at the loss
of human sensitivity.

If the mother goat's wisdom represents the source of the Earth's creation, then the seven little goats can be seen as the multiple dimensions of the Earth's wholeness. They can be thought of as seven complete spheres where different evolutions, connected to either the Earth or to the Universe, have found an ideal place to live and evolve. Some of them are embodied in material form, while others exist on more subtle levels, making them invisible to the physical eye. In one such spherical space, for example, the souls of humanity dwell between two incarnations. In another, the world of elemental beings evolves and works from there in the nature and landscapes of the Earth. The third spherical space is the home to the elven race called 'Sidhe' (pronounced 'shee') in Celtic tradition and 'Ajdi' in Slovenian native tradition. The fourth sphere could be the home of the archetypal souls of the various animal species, and so on up to the mythical number seven. The tale suggests that such a multi-dimensional space of the Earth exists, symbolized in the hiding places of each of the seven little goats in a different micro-space of the goat house – with the latter representing a coherent whole, best called 'Earth's Universe'.

Not long after, the mother goat comes back from the woods to find everything at home upside down. The front door is wide open, the table and chairs thrown about, the sink lies broken in pieces on the floor, the quilts and pillows pulled off the bed. She calls the children by name one after the other, but no one answers. When she comes to the seventh name, the youngest goat cries with a soft voice, "Here I am, mother, hiding in the clock case." She helps her out and learns that the wolf has come and eaten all her sisters.

Desperate, the mother goat runs around the house looking for the wolf, until she spots him lying under a tree, snoring after his big feast. She cautiously approaches him and notices something moving and jiggling inside his full belly.

To avoid getting lost in the suspenseful story, let's start again from the beginning. Both in the Universe and on Earth, the decision needs to be made again and again as to which path of development to follow. The wisdom of the Earth uses the image of the seven little goats to mark a path based on loving and caring intelligence and the inclusive principle. The wolf, by contrast, advocates a path of strict order based on rational logic and the exclusion of difference. With the help of human carelessness and fear – think of the baker and the miller – the 'wolf' forces have succeeded in invading the Earth's multidimensional space and disrupting its order, based on the autonomy of individual evolutions and on the common purpose of evolving the principle of life to ever-greater perfection and beauty.

At this point of the fairy tale, it seems that the forces of darkness have triumphed. But not really: the little goat hidden in the clock case survived the intrusion. The tale thus confirms that there are cosmic cycles, here represented by the rhythmic ticking of the clockwork, which do not allow love and kindness to be defeated forever. When the cycle of a particular experience is reversed, the door to a new experience of life opens.

And that is what happened. The little goat has to run home and fetch scissors, needle and thread. The mother goat then cuts open the full belly of the beast, and the first little goat sticks her head out. As she continues to cut, all six young goats jump out of its belly, alive and unhurt. How happy they were! The mother sends the children in search of seven heavy stones to fill the wicked beast's belly with while he is still asleep and snoring. Then the goat sews it up again, so that he didn't notice anything and never once stirred.

It was this scene that made me decide to include the story of the wolf and the seven little goats in this book of Grimm's fairy tales for adults. In recent decades I have noticed that the single-layered space created and anchored in the human consciousness by the rational mind has begun to open up. A new cycle of evolution of the Earth and the Universe has begun. Gaia, the creator of the Earth, is cutting the armour in which (in the wolf's belly) the multi-layered space of existence has been enclosed and blocked.

First, we began to understand the existence of the vital-energy network of the landscape with its centres of life force. Then we became aware of the sacred dimensions of the Earth and its landscapes. The various beings of the invisible worlds of the Earth have emerged to the surface of our sensitivity. A community begins to form in which the different evolutions of the Earth and of the Universe are united... But what is happening to the wolf?

When the wolf finally gets enough sleep, he stands up on his legs and feels a strange weight in his stomach. The stones make him thirsty so he rushes to a nearby well to drink. When he walks there, the stones in his stomach move about and knock against each other. He says: "I have swallowed six little goats, and now they are as heavy as stones." He leans over the edge of the well and the weight of the stones pulls him in. He stumbles into the water and drowns.

The tale envisions two stages in the transformation of the opposing forces that sought to triumph over the freedom of life. In the first stage, they are taken in by deep layers of minerals (stones). Embedded in the mineral tissues, these unfortunate creatures will undergo a transformation that will possibly last millions of years until they are purified. In the second phase, the memory of their past violence, now purified of poison, flows into the memory of the oceans in the interior of the Earth. Water is the guardian of memory and wisdom, which even now tries to protects humanity and the Earth from the hidden intrusion of life-opposing forces and beings.

Embedded in the mineral tissues of
the rocks, the life-opposing forces
are undergoing transformation.

Cinderella

Unlike the other stories collected so far, Cinderella focuses on processes of actual cosmic changes as manifesting within the personal human being. It speaks of the schism within the human being in an age of patriarchal domination. Broken into several disconnected parts, human beings have found themselves at the point of forgetting their original wholeness.

The story begins with the death of Cinderella's mother and her mourning over the loss. The death of the beloved mother points to the tragic situation that is partly still relevant for the current state of human development. In order to gradually rise to the level of deeper and more conscious connectedness and wholeness, human beings had temporarily to give up the Gaia's protection and care, our beloved planetary mother. We had to forget our wonderful previous oneness with the life-currents of the Earth and detach ourselves from the motherly arms of the Goddess, which have cradled us during past periods of evolution. Only then, left alone in the face of life's challenges could we hope to reach the stage of spiritual and mental adulthood – which should be the characteristic of the present epoch of our evolution.

In the case of Cinderella, her mother's death marks the above-described tragic breaking point in the evolution of humanity, which historically took place at the end of the Neolithic period some 5,000 years ago. We have found ourselves in a male-led civilisation, characterised by a deepening state of internal human schism.

The unfortunate break starts to manifest with the father's decision to find another wife. The new wife, Cinderella's stepmother brings not just one, but two daughters into the family. In the fairy-tale language, they are described with the attributes "sweet and fair-faced, but with evil and dark hearts". They obviously symbolise a step away from oneness or a step towards dualism. This is expressed in the difference between the qualities of human existence as they are manifested externally or internally, in the form of a division between the positive and the negative side, and finally in the oscillation between the material and the spiritual dimensions of being. The two newly arrived daughters symbolise the polarised attitude to life that has become the dominant worldview since the Goddess withdrew from the celestial sphere of human cultures. The original cyclical connection to the world whole, embodied in the figure of the Neolithic Goddess, has been replaced by a social order based on the principles of division, accumulation of power and separation.

In the figurative language of the tale, the principle of separation is expressed in the form of Cinderella's different family status in relation to her two half-sisters. Cinderella had to "work hard, get up before daybreak, carry water, fire up the stove, cook and wash". The stepmother's daughters, on the other hand, jumped at any chance to avoid their obligations. Nevertheless, they were allowed to sleep in the white bed, while Cinderella slept in the ashes under the hearth.

One day Cinderella's father goes to a fair in a nearby town and asks the stepdaughters what he should bring them from the town. "Beautiful dresses," said the first. "Pearls and jewels," said the second. "And you, Cinderella," says the father, "what do you want?" "Bring me the first hazel twig, dear father, that brushes against your hat on your way home."

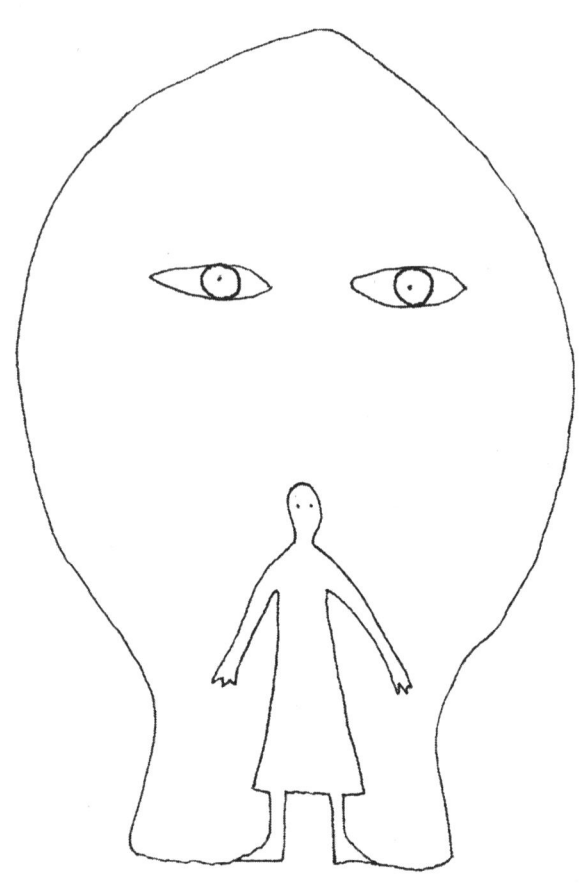

Cinderella never lost touch
with her late mother.

He indeed bought the stepdaughters beautiful dresses and jewels. On his way home, as he was riding through the green thicket, a hazel twig brushed against him and knocked off his hat. He broke it off and brought it to Cinderella.

The father's question before he sets off for the city, as to what he should bring the three girls as a gift, reveals the depth of the schism into which the modern human being has fallen. In line with their egocentric ideals, the half-sisters wanted beautiful dresses and jewels. Cinderella, on the other hand, trusting in the wisdom of nature, asked her father to bring her a simple hazel twig. It is no coincidence that Cinderella chose the hazel twig. Such twigs were used by medieval geomancers for dowsing and for discovering underground water sources. Hazel twigs were also often used as so-called 'magic wands'. And she did not ask for just any hazel whip, but the one that had revealed itself to be of a fairy quality by knocking off her father's hat.

As a reward for her trust in the powers of nature, Cinderella was given a hazel twig with magic powers. She planted it on her mother's grave and watered it with her tears. "And behold, the twig took hold and grew into a beautiful tree." Whatever she wished for under the tree was granted. Translated into linear language, this means that Cinderella embodies that part of the divided human being that has been pushed into the subconscious and remains this way connected to the elemental cycle of birth, death and the rebirth of life, and thus shares in its magic powers.

Cinderella goes to the grave three times every day and talks in silence with her dead mother, who now lives in the world of ancestors and descendants, in the so-called 'spiritual world'. In response to the trust Cinderella has in her mother, knowing that she is not dead but alive in the afterlife, when called, a white bird would approach the hazel tree. When Cinderella makes a wish, the bird, as a symbol of the mother dwelling in the world of souls, throws down to her whatever she has wished for.

In order not to get lost among the fairy tale images, I would like to present my key to Cinderella, which is this: all the characters in the fairy tale represent individual parts of the once whole, but nowadays fragmented, human being:

Together, the father and the deceased mother symbolise the divine embrace within which the cycle of the human being, oscillating between earthly life and afterlife, takes place. In the journey of souls, the father represents the phase of living in the embodied world among fellow human beings, stones, plants, animals and the landscapes of the Earth. The deceased mother represents the complementary part of the cycle that takes place in the etheric world as life after life. Both are alive, but each in a different way – a destiny shared by all members of the human race.

However, in the circumstances of the patriarchal age – also called the 'Iron Age' by historians – the mother was replaced by the stepmother, a symbol of religious concepts, social norms and psychological patterns invented by the power of the human mind, which gradually replaced humanity's direct relationship with the beings of life and its multidimensionality. Instead of living in the immediacy of his connection with the totality of life, modern human beings, under the influence of the 'stepmother', succumb to the artificial filters and masks that define the horizon of our narrowed reality.

Cinderella's two half-sisters embody the consequences of this process of self-alienation. They symbolise the fragmented and isolated part of the personality that modern people call the 'ego'. Just as the two intruders flaunt their external glamour, taking control of Cinderella's house, so the external self (ego) tries to take control over modern people's thoughts and actions. The problem is that the ego, entangled in its superficiality and one-sidedness, cannot provide people with inner stability, peace and grounding, let alone a spiritual foundation for existence. We are therefore destined to oscillate between faith and doubt,

The hazel twig has taken hold
and grown into a magic tree.

between hatred and love, between enthusiasm for spirituality and devotion to materialism.

The only aspect that could provide the human being with mental stability, with grounding and a spiritual foundation is our true, yet nowadays ignored, Self. In the story, the Self is given the name 'Cinderella' because it has to settle for a bed of cinders instead of a proper bed. The cinders are the remnants of the fire that once burned in the light of consciousness, clearly visible to everyone. As much as sleeping in a white bed might signify the human being bathed in the light of consciousness, sleeping in cinders symbolises being suppressed into the subconscious realms. Cinderella, then, represents the original Self of the human being that has been pushed into the subconscious from where, unacknowledged, humiliated and repressed, it inspires in a hidden way the process of human liberation and reconnection to the whole.

The story then introduces a fourth element of human inner space. It is represented by the royal castle, elevated above the landscape of the everyday reality. It is represented by the prince as a symbol of the human essence, dwelling beyond the constraints of linear space and time. I equate the king's son with the 'son or daughter of the Divinity', that is, with the concept of human all-encompassing or divine self. At this level, the human being does not enter into the cycle of birth, life, death, afterlife and rebirth. The divine self is the core of human identity, residing in eternity as the foundation of the individual's unique wholeness.

This highest level of the human being is introduced into the story by the king himself, when he calls a great feast in the name of his son and invites all the beauties of his land, so that his son, the prince, could find the most beautiful bride. The stepsisters were also invited to the feast together with their mother. They call Cinderella, saying: "Comb our hair, brush our shoes and fasten our shiny buckles. We are going to the wedding at the royal castle!" Cinderella obeys, but sheds bitter tears because she too would like to go to the ball. She begs her stepmother to allow her to go, but she replies, "You, Cinderella, all covered with dust and dirt, what would you like to go to the ball for? You have neither clothes nor shoes to dance in!" But Cinderella keeps asking, so the stepmother scatters a bowl of peas into the ashes and promises to take her to the ball if she picks the peas out of the ashes in two hours.

The king's call to prepare for the wedding of his only son can be felt as a foreshadowing of a fateful turning point in human history. In the form of a wedding, it predicts the possibility of reuniting the fragmented parts of the human being into a whole. In this sense, the king's son represents the archetype of a human being who knows the complex path of human fulfilment. He knows beyond any doubt that the time of our exclusion from the totality of life, which took place under the conditions of the Iron Age, is coming to an end. Its purpose is fulfilled, the process of humanity's ever-deepening isolation is complete. The time of fundamental change is approaching, and with it the necessity of reintegration into the whole. The king's son is already seeking to bring the dispersed elements of the human whole into the embrace of a common being. In the language of the tale, he announces his decision to marry and organises three feasts dedicated to choosing the right bride.

But before the process of 'marriage' between the fragmented parts of human wholeness can begin, the test of personal readiness for such an epochal undertaking must be passed. The fairy tale therefore introduces two tests that Cinderella must pass if she is to make it to the grand ball that the king's son plans to give to discover his true bride. To test her, the stepmother scatters first peas and then lentils into the ashes under the hearth and demands that she pick every last grain from the ashes. Translated into colloquial language, the test would mean that in the preparatory period one must learn to separate the life-bearing sprouts of the future from the dead remains of the past. The seeds symbolise the former, the ashes the latter. The spirit of the Iron Age – which Hindus call Kali Yuga – embodied in the stepmother, deliberately confused a person's inner self (mixing the seeds with the ashes) in order to challenge his will to spiritual progress and growth.

Cinderella did not find the ordeal difficult because she has never lost her attunement to the wholeness of life. In response to her all-connectedness, three species of birds come to her rescue: white pigeons, turtledoves and a "swarm of birds from beneath the sky". They represent the three different powers available to human beings as the sons/daughters of Sister Earth, but given to us only on condition that we maintain and nurture our elemental relationship with the wisdom of the Earth and nature. The pigeons can be interpreted as symbols of feminine spiritual powers, the turtledoves as the emotional values of the elemental world, and the birds of the sky as intuition.

Despite having passed both tests, Cinderella's stepmother refuses to take her to the feast. She turns her back on Cinderella and hurries away with her two daughters on her arm. As soon as they are gone, Cinderella goes to her mother's grave under the hazel tree and cries out: "Shake and quiver, little tree, Throw gold and silver down to me!"

The tree, as an expression of her late mother, answers by throwing down a silver and gold dress and a pair of shoes embroidered with gold and silver. She quickly puts on the dress and runs off to the ball. Her stepmother and her half-sisters do not recognise her, thinking that she is sitting at home, picking lentils from the ashes.

The prince quickly spots her, approaches her and asks her to dance. He couldn't bear to leave her side and danced with her until late in the evening. When she leaves, he wants to escort her home to find out where she came from. However, she slips away and hides by jumping into a pigeon coop. The prince runs for

The prince recognises the dancer
as his bride-to-be, but her origins
remain hidden from him.

the axe and cuts the pigeon coop in two, but finds no one inside. Cinderella has miraculously disappeared. When the stepmother and the girls return from the feast, they find her asleep in the ashes under the hearth.

The prince recognises his true bride at first sight, but the time is not yet ripe for a lasting union. Even the king's son has yet to pave his way to reconnection and break down the barriers put in place during the period of alienation, on a path that leads to the embrace of wholeness. The figurative language of the tale represents the first obstacle with the image of the pigeon coop where Cinderella has hidden herself in order to conceal her true identity. The pigeon coop could represent a fluttering collection of emotional tendencies characteristic of a modern person's relationship to nature and the Earth. I would characterise it by an exuberant love for all that is alive and beautiful, but lacking a deep, multi-faceted view. It lacks the free will to accept, love and cherish the Earth and nature in their primordial otherness, independent of the human mind.

During the feast the next night, Cinderella escapes to hide in "a beautiful tall tree full of magnificent pears". Let us suppose that the pear tree symbolises the Earth's life forces, which can become an obstacle in the evolutionary path of humanity and the planet if they are misunderstood and misused. An example is the misplaced focus of our civilisation on the purely material fertility of the soil, which then falls victim to various techniques of blackmail. Conversely, it refuses to see or even hinders the health of the Earth's vital tissue on the vital-energetic, emotional and spiritual levels. The prince orders the pear tree to be cut down to indicate the necessity of outgrowing the one-sided tendency towards fertility and material abundance, with concomitant deprivation on the other levels of existence – but he does not find his mate on it.

Before the third ball, the prince sets a trap for his chosen but still unidentified bride. He has the stairs she has fled down each time smeared with pitch. When the beauty slips out of his hands for the third time and runs away to reach her bed by the hearth in time, she loses one of her golden shoes. It is stuck in the pitch. This finally gives the son the key to his true bride.

This brings about the final act in the process of reconnecting the fragmented parts of the human being into a whole. Meanwhile, the obstacles on both sides have been removed, and the spiritual self can now 'embody more deeply', that is, connect more closely with its partner, the elemental aspect of the self, connected with the life of the Earth. The story portrays the new circumstances with the image of the king's son descending from the castle heights and appearing unexpectedly at the door of the 'Earth family' to announce his decision:

"No one shall be my wife except for the one whose foot fits this golden shoe."

As a representative of the dominant social and cultural norms, the stepmother is convinced that only one of her two daughters, the representatives of the superficial ego, is fit for the role of bride. She retreats to be alone with the older daughter and tries in vain to fit the fateful shoe on her foot. "But she could not get her big toe into it, for the golden shoe was too small for her." Her mother advised her: "Cut off your toe, and when you are queen you will no longer have to walk." The deception is revealed during the ride to the castle when blood starts dripping from the shoe. A similar thing happens to the younger sister after she cuts off her heel to put on her shoe.

I associate the shoe, marked with a specific dimension (number) corresponding to a certain individual, with the personal code of the individualised person. It symbolises the archetype of the human being, stored in the Earth's memory. As such, it represents the archetypal framework of a particular human being valid for each of his incarnations. The archetype ensures the uniqueness of the individual being, which must not fade or be lost from one incarnation to the next. It has a decisive

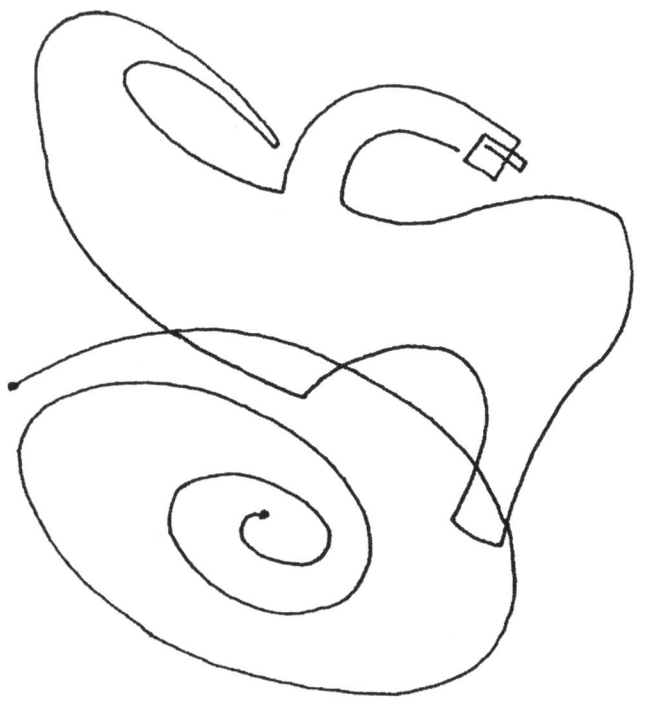

A mysterious dancer has
lost her golden shoe.

influence on the quality of one's personal relationships with the life systems and beings of the Earth. As such, the archetype inscribed in the memory of the Earth complements the human soul-self and is the elementary pole of our identity. The golden shoe is a fitting symbol for it.

After the bitter realisation that the second daughter is not the right bride either, the prince asks his father if he might have a third daughter. He reluctantly acknowledges that there is a Cinderella in the house and immediately degrades her by saying: "There is only a deformed little Cinderella from my late first wife." The prince insists on trying the shoe on her too, and lo and behold, Cinderella's golden shoe fits like a glove! The discovered bride rides to the castle with the prince.

Let us compare the prince's search for the right bride with the stages of human evolution. As we have become increasingly alienated from the delicate existential and conscious dimensions of the Earth over the past millennia, we have also gradually lost touch with the archetypes that control the multidimensional lifestreams on the planet. The result is a weakening and dilution of human groundedness at different levels of being, which is in horrific contradiction to the earthly character of human existence, which is valid as long as we are developing as an evolution on and in communication with the Earth.

In fact, the conscious connection with earthly wholeness has been lost by that aspect of the detached personality which is usually called the 'ego'. It is no longer able to put on the golden shoe, as was the case with Cinderella's two half-sisters. Even the attempt to fool the prince by an apparent grounding does not help them, just as modern civilisation cannot be helped in solving ecological problems by its apparent grounding in materialism. It gives the impression that we have penetrated deeper into earthly nature than any culture before us and that we are constantly dealing with materialized reality. But in fact, we are dealing only with the most superficial layer of earthly existence, with everything essential remaining denied, like Cinderella is denied in the fairy tale. I am referring to the vital organism of the Earth, its elementary consciousness, its emotional level and its divine essence.

If the modern human being were to try on his own 'shoe' – which is necessary if we are to begin the process of reconnecting the broken parts of the human being – it would become tragically apparent that the Earth no longer recognises us as part of its whole. Cutting off a toe at the front or a heel at the back does not help.

But the message of the tale of Cinderella should in no way be seen as a threat, in the sense that the prince will come as a divine judge to separate those who have remained faithful to Sister Earth from those who have lost touch with her. It should not be overlooked that all the characters in the tale represent parts of a single human being who, in the process of human evolution, have become alienated from one another or even found themselves in opposition to each other. Therefore, none of them can be cursed or rejected without the one who utters the curse mutilating himself.

Rather, the Cinderella message is aimed at making people aware of the significance of their own 'Cinderella' for their personal development, which is already valid today, but which is above all future-oriented. The one-sided worldview of the Iron Age increasingly tabooed and demeaned the relationship to the 'Earth within' symbolised by Cinderella. The elemental essence of the human being had no choice but to dwell in the dark realm of the subconscious. Its forces are considered esoteric waste, worthy of the dustbin of the social unconscious.

But alas! When the evolution of the human being moves into the phase of reconnecting its own dispersed parts, it will be rough. The reconnection between the angelic and the elemental human being within us can only be realised on the basis of the archetype which is encoded on the sub-elemental level and in which the key of belonging to each other has been enshrined since the beginning of our embodiment on Earth. In the face of humanity's degeneration in relation to the archetypes of being, the future fusion of the parts of our being is only possible if we wake up in time from the slumber of our self-alienation and choose our 'Cinderella' as the cornerstone of our new identity.

As the prince leads Cinderella to her wedding, the two white pigeons perch on her shoulders. As is the case with the daughter of the archetypal Goddess, one perched on her left shoulder, the other on her right. Her two half-sisters also accompanied her to the wedding, the older one on her right side, the younger one on her left. The pigeons peck out one eye from each of them. When the procession was returning from the wedding, they walked the other way round, the younger on the right and the older one on the left, and then the pigeons pecked out the other eye from each of them. They became blind, which I see as a symbol of the abolition of the one-sided, 'blind' view of life.

But I would like to point out that this is not about revenge. The loss of the left and right eyes, i.e. the blinding, symbolises the transformation of an aspect of the human being that is detached from the whole and which is called the 'ego'. It now works, as befits its true role, alongside the true human self, which has risen like a phoenix from the ashes of oblivion. Cinderella has not rejected the transformed ego, but has invited it into her reassembled wholeness.

Rumpelstiltskin

Once upon a time there was a miller who was poor but had a beautiful daughter. One day, a king came by and got into a conversation with the miller. The miller, trying to make a good impression, said to him, "I have a daughter who can spin straw into gold."

"Wow!" the king marveled, "now that is an art I like! If your daughter is really as clever as you say, bring her to my castle tomorrow. I will put her to the test."

The next day the miller brought the girl to the castle. They took her to a room filled with straw. The king brought a spinning wheel and a reel and said, "Get to work. If by morning you have not spun this straw into gold, then you will have to die." He locked the room and left the girl alone in it.

The poor miller's daughter had no idea how to spin straw into gold. She became more and more afraid, and at last began to cry bitterly.

The first chapter is a moving illustration of the disconnect between the ambitions of the human race and the reality of the situation in which humanity finds itself today. On the one hand, humanity, like the poor miller, boasts about how we are conquering space with our rockets and walking on Mars. On the other hand, we are unable to keep peace on Earth and are leaving a large part of humanity to hunger and poverty. The father claims that his daughter can turn straw into gold, but the daughter has no idea how to make the transformation that medieval alchemists called 'the transformation of lead into gold' and scientists refer to as a 'quantum leap' from one level of existence to another.

Is there even a possibility to take on such a challenge? Obviously not at the level of ordinary consciousness.

All at once, the door opens and in comes a strange little man, saying, "Young Miss Miller, why are you crying so miserably?"

"I have to spin straw into gold, and I do not know how to do it," cries the girl.

"What will you give me if I spin it for you?" asks the little man.

"I'll give you my necklace," replies the girl.

The little man took the necklace, sat down before the spinning wheel, and whir, whir, whir, three times pulled, and the spool was full. Then he put another one on, and whir, whir, whir, three times pulled, and the second one was full as well. And so it went on until the next morning, until all the straw was spun and all the spools were filled with gold.

At sunrise, the king arrives. When he sees all the gold, he gets greedy and wants more. The next evening, he has the young miller girl taken to an even bigger room filled with straw, ordering her to spin it into gold if she valued her life.

The story repeats itself. The girl couldn't help herself and sobbed bitterly. Once again, the door opens, and the little man appears. He asks the young miller what will she give him if he spins her straw into gold. The poor miller has only a ring on her hand and gives it to him. The man takes the ring, starts the wheel and by morning spins all the straw into glistening gold.

At this point, we cannot yet know who the mysterious little man is who has the uncanny ability to turn straw into gold. However, since he responds to the young woman's moaning and puts on her necklace and ring, we can imagine that he is not something completely alien to her, but rather a force

The unfortunate miller's daughter
has no idea how to turn a
roomful of straw into gold.

mysteriously connected to humanity. The ring and the necklace are symbols of such a connection. The link, however, is apparently unknown, lying forgotten in the human subconscious.

It is also interesting that it is straw that he transforms into gold. The latter, with its golden yellow colour, resembles gold, but is infinitely far from the precious quality of it. We can therefore assume that the relationship between the girl and the little man is about a completely forgotten human creative faculty, which, if it could be redeemed from oblivion, would enable the human being to 'move mountains'.

But as the story goes on, we are reminded that this creative faculty can also be disastrous when used in combination with one's will to power and wealth. The first reminder of this is the king's greed for gold.

The king comes back in the morning, amazed at the riches the beautiful miller made for him. He takes her to a third, even larger room with straw and offers her to be his wife if she spins a third room of straw. "So what if she is a miller's daughter," he says to himself, "I could not find a richer wife in the whole world."

When the girl is left crying alone with the straw, the little man comes back and asks, "What will you give me if I spin the straw for you this time also?"

"I have nothing more to give you," the girl replies.

"Then promise me, if you should become queen, to give me your first child."

The unfortunate girl didn't know how else to help herself. She promised the little man what he asked for, and he once again spun all the straw into gold.

The king was a man of his word and did indeed marry the girl. And the beautiful miller's daughter became queen. A year later she gave birth to a beautiful child, and she thought no more of the strange little man. But one day he appeared in her room and demanded for himself what she had promised him.

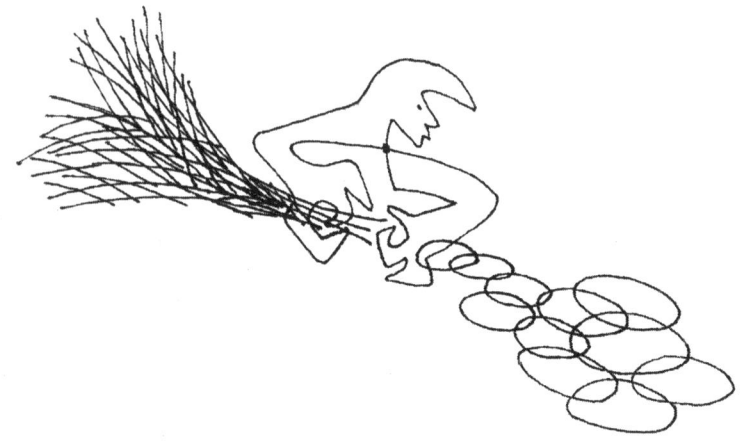

The little man sat down at the wheel, spun it and the straw began to turn to gold.

The queen was horrorstruck and offers the little man all the wealth of the kingdom if he would let her keep the child. He says: "No, something alive is dearer to me than all the treasures in the world." Then the queen began to lament and cry so heartbreakingly the little man took pity on her. "I will give you three days," he said to her, "and if by then you know my name, then you shall keep your child."

The strange little man has already shown mercy to the unfortunate girl three times, which is why we cannot attribute to him a diabolical nature, although he is capable of acts far beyond the common capacity of human creativity. The mystery of his identity revolves around his name, which can be understood as a question about his place in the mosaic of different aspects that make up the totality of the Earth's Universe. The latter goes beyond the constraints of space and time. A name is a sign of the essence of a particular being.

The queen spent the entire night thinking of all the names she had ever heard. Then she sent a messenger into the country to inquire far and wide for any other names that there might be. When the little man returned the next day, she began with Caspar, Melchior, Balthazar, and said all the names she knew, one after another, but after each one the little man said, "That is not my name." On the second day she had inquiries made in faraway lands as to the names of the people there. She gave the little man the most uncommon and curious names. "Perhaps your name is Shortribs, or Sheepshanks, or Laceleg?" But the little man always answered, "No, that is not my name."

This passage is relevant to our question about the identity of the strange little man – even if only in a negative sense. All we learn is that human names don't fit him, and neither do the names of things. The little man, then, does not belong to the human world as we know it in terms of his outward appearances perceptible with the five senses. His place is neither among men nor among things.

Where else, then, can we look for its origin?

On the third day the messenger returns and says, "I have not been able to find a single new name. But when I was approaching a high mountain in the corner of the woods, there where the fox and the hare say good-night to each other, I saw a little house. A fire was burning in the yard, and quite a ridiculous man was jumping around the fire, hopping on one leg and singing:

'Today I'll bake; tomorrow I'll brew,

Then I'll fetch the queen's new child,

It is good that no one knows,

Rumpelstiltskin is my name.'"

If we listen carefully to the narrative of the queen's messenger, we can learn a lot about the strange little man's home and origins. The messenger mentions a high mountain and a "corner of the woods". From the point of view of geomancy, as the science of the multidimensionality of space, both are signs of a sacred place. "On top of a mountain" means that the place is close to the spiritual dimensions of existence. And "corner of the woods" is a description of the dimensions of space that exists beyond the realm of rational explanation or sensory perception.

Even more revealing is the observation that "there [...] the fox and the hare say good-night to each other". Given that the fox and the hare are known as adversaries, and that the fox eats the hare, we are clearly dealing with a dimension of space where the normal rules of life do not apply. We are dealing with a dimension of space marked by harmony between opposites.

These are all signs of the dimension of Earth's creation that tradition calls the 'fairy world'. This does not refer to the world of elemental beings, as in the case of the tale of the Frog King. Elemental beings guide and shape the lifestreams of nature; this also applies to human beings, but only in so far as we are part of the fabric of nature. Rather, it is the story of Sleeping Beauty and the thirteen fates that gives the fairy beings their proper place in the mosaic of Earth's creatures. Folk tradition describes them as mediators between the Mother of Life and the human race. It describes their ability to help people with illnesses and to teach them the art of handicraft and healing.

In the tradition of the Italian Dolomites, the fairy beings are called 'Fanes'. Today, the Celtic name 'Sidhe' (pronounced 'shee') is most commonly used for them, a name preserved in Irish tradition.

The next morning, the strange little man came again and asked, "Well, Lady Queen, what is my name?" The queen refuses to reveal that she knows his real name and asks jokingly, "Is your name Conrad, by any chance? Or is it Harry?" "No!" Then, with special emphasis, she says, "Might your name perhaps be Rumpelstiltskin?"

The little man turned green with anger, and stomped his left foot so hard into the ground that he sank into it.

Looking again at the story of Rumpelstiltskin, we can see two levels of relations between the fairy and the human race. The first two nights, when the little man spun straw into gold, represent a period in human history when there was still an awareness of the presence of fairy beings. People used to bring small gifts to the places of their dwelling, worshipped and respected them. The necklace and ring given to Rumpelstiltskin by the beautiful miller are symbolic of this indigenous-inspired period. In Slovenia, it survived in the form of so-called 'Old Belief' until the middle of the 20th century.

The plot with the third room filled with straw and the queen's child is a visionary reference to the period we are living in today. Human rationality, in the form of scientific research into the human genome, has, speaking symbolically, penetrated into the hidden little house where Rumpelstiltskin lives and revealed his 'name'. It has decoded human DNA and established a firm public belief that there is no secret link between humans and parallel worlds of Earth, such as the fairy world.

Rumpelstiltskin sank into the ground.

Hansel and Gretel

On the edge of a vast forest lived a poor woodcutter with his second wife and his two children. The boy's name was Hansel and the girl's name was Gretel. The woodcutter's family already had little to eat, and once, when a great famine came to the land, he could no longer provide even their daily bread.

One night as he was lying in bed worrying about his problems, he sighed and said to his wife, "What is to become of us? How can we feed our children when we have nothing for ourselves?"

"You know what," replies the wife, "early tomorrow morning we will take the children into the thickest part of the woods. We'll make a fire, give them each a little piece of bread, and then we'll go and chop firewood and leave them alone. That way they will never find their way home again, and we will be rid of them."

"No, wife," says the husband, "I will not do that. I cannot bring myself to abandon my own children alone in the woods. Wild beasts would come and tear them apart."

"Oh, you fool," says the wife, "then you think all four of us should starve to death. All we can do is to plane the boards for our coffins." And she gives him no peace until the father agrees.

The two children, too, could not sleep because of their hunger, and they heard what the stepmother had said to the father.

The story of Hansel and Gretel, dressed up in fairy-tale imagery, reminds us that the ways of gaining knowledge about the secrets of life, those used by human communities for millennia, are blocked. I am referring to the paths of initiation, that is, of direct introduction to the mysteries of existence in the earthly world. People did not go to schools, but went to particular places in nature where they could get the necessary inner experiences. They helped them to live in the embodied world in such a way that their lives were meaningful and fulfilled.

There is another way of being initiated into the mysteries of being. I am referring to pilgrimages to places where individuals could listen to the teachings of enlightened women and men, perhaps by living with them for a while, serving them and gaining knowledge by talking to them or simply by co-existing with them in a way that was full of meaning and light.

But gone are the days when the ways of the ancestors could be trusted. In the meantime, the stepmother has replaced the Mother of Life in the role of caretaker, responsible for the circumstances within which humanity's life on Earth is meant to be meaningful and blessed. As a patriarchal disguise of the mother, the stepmother is primarily concerned with her own survival and benefit. There is no longer a selfless tribal community to ensure that no one in the human family goes hungry and destitute.

Hansel says to Gretel: "Don't cry, I'll think of something." As soon as the old couple have fallen asleep, he sneaks out of the cottage and collects pockets full of pebbles. The moon helps him, because the white pebbles glisten like silver coins in the moonlight.

Early in the morning, before sunrise, the stepmother comes and wakes the two children. "Get up, you lazybones, we're going into the woods to fetch wood." She gave them each a piece of bread, saying, "Here is something for lunch, but don't eat it before, because you won't get anything else."

On the way to the forest, Hansel walks at the back of the line. Now and then he stops and looks back, as if he is saying goodbye to his home, but in fact he is taking white pebbles from his pocket and dropping them on the path. They camp in the middle of the forest and make a big fire. "Now, children, lie down by the fire and rest," says the stepmother. "Father and I are going into the woods to cut wood. When we are finished, we will come back for you."

But they didn't come back. The children fell sound asleep by the fire and woke up in the middle of the night, left on their own. Gretel begins to cry, saying, "How are we going to get out of the dark woods now?" "Just wait a little for the moon to rise and show us the way," Hansel comforts her. When the moon was high in the sky, Hansel took Gretel by the hand and guided her towards home, following the white pebbles that glistened like newly minted coins, showing them the way. They walked all night and only arrived back at their cottage at dawn the next day.

Life in the conditions of the material world is not easy for the human soul, accustomed to the ethereal spaces of existence where we exist between death and rebirth. When embodied on Earth – we discussed this in the chapter on the Frog King – the human being feels lost. And yet we ourselves have chosen the challenges of embodied life as a condition of our inner growth and development. We are comforted by the story of the Frog King, which tells us that elemental beings are there to help us cope with the conditions of matter.

The story of Hansel and Gretel comforts us in another way. It addresses the other half of the human race, which is not currently embodied, but observes life on Earth from the sphere of the spiritual world. Unburdened by the relative narrowness of matter, the perspective of the souls of ancestors and posterity is much wider. They can foresee the possible obstacles and false steps on the path of the individual human being through the thicket of embodied life. The white stones that sparkle like silver

In the moonlight, the pebbles
glistened like silver coins,
showing the way.

coins are the manifestation of their guidance, which human beings are able to perceive intuitively and to some extent consciously. They guide them safely through life.

A few weeks passed, and the whole country was again stricken with great scarcity. And once more the children heard their stepmother say to their father in bed at night: "We are almost out of food. The children must go. We will take them deeper into the woods, so they will not find their way out. Otherwise, there will be no help for us." The father felt sad at heart, but the wife would listen to nothing that he said. The children were awake and had overheard the entire conversation. Hansel got up again and wanted to collect pebbles as he had done before. But this time the cunning stepmother had locked the door, and Hansel could not get out.

Luckily, they each got a little piece of bread for their lunch, so instead of using pebbles, Hansel marked the way with bread crumbs. The story repeats itself and the two children wake up alone again in the middle of an unknown forest. They wait for moonlight so they can see the bread crumbs and follow them on their way home.

When the moon rose, they got up and set off on their journey home, but they could not find any crumbs. The birds had eaten them all up. "We'll find our way anyway," Hansel comforted his sister. But they did not find it. They walked all night and all the next day, but they did not find their way out of the woods. They were terribly hungry and so tired that their legs would no longer carry them. They lay down under a big tree and fell asleep hungry.

The birds did not want to do Hansel and Gretel any harm by eating the bread crumbs. They were only warning modern human beings that the motivations of the guidance that had previously flowed so freely from the world of ancestors and descendants were no longer reliable. A fog of mutual distrust has been cast, as a result of an ethically distorted patriarchal civilisation oriented towards the power of the individual and of nations. The stepmother locked the door so that Hansel could not collect the pebbles. But perhaps it is still possible to find a holistic way through life with the help of enlightened individuals, healers, seers and those rare individuals who understand the magic of the consecrated life and are therefore rightly called wizards or witches?

Gretel and Hansel woke up on the third morning since they had left home. They started walking again, but only wandered deeper and deeper into the woods. They felt that if help had not come soon, they would have collapsed and died. Around midday, they saw a little snow-white bird sitting on a branch. It sang so beautifully that they stopped and listened to it. When it was finished, it spread its wings and flew from branch to branch in front of them. They followed the bird until it led them to a strange little house and sat on the roof. As they approached the house, they were astonished to find that it was made of bread and covered with walnut dumplings, with windows made of sugar bars. They immediately began to feast on the treats. Hansel nibbled on a piece of bread from the roof, and Gretel started to eat the sweet window panes.

Then a gentle voice called out from inside:

"Nibble, nibble, little mouse,

Who is nibbling at my house?"

The children replied, "The wind so wild, the heavenly child," and continued to eat, without being distracted. Suddenly the door opened. A woman, hunched over and as old as the Earth, comes out of the house, leaning on a crutch.

The alternative path to the truth opens with the white bird, which appears before Gretel and Hansel as a harbinger of the wisdom of Gaia, the mother of the earthly universe. The bird jumps from branch to branch and leads them to a small house where they not only find food for their stomachs, but also meet a wise old woman. What is typical here is that the two children, as seekers of truth and love, first meet the old woman on a telepathic level, in the form of a cordial dialogue with her – even before they see her. Contact is first established on the level of the natural elements of life (the mouse nibbles and the wind blows). We are obviously dealing with an introduction (initiation) into the mysteries of existence on the basis of the wisdom of the Earth and its elemental worlds – as opposed to the initiation on the basis of contact with the ancestors and descendants described above.

"Oh, you dear children, who brought you here?" said the woman. "Just come in and stay with me. No harm will come to you." She took them by the hand, led them into the house and served them a delicious lunch. She made them two white beds. Hansel and Gretel lay down and fell asleep.

But the old woman had only pretended to be friendly. She was a wicked witch who preyed on the children and had built her house of bread just to lure them to her. But when a child fell into her trap, she would kill him, cook him, and eat him.

At this unpleasant point, the tale reminds the seekers of truth and contact with the essence of life that with the dominance of the rational worldview in the era of the Renaissance, a dangerous collapse known as the 'witch-hunt' had taken place. It began with the Papal Encyclical of 1496, calling for the persecution of so-called 'witches', and ended only with the period of the so-called Enlightenment at the end of the 18th century. Over a period of three centuries, an unknown but awfully large number of wise women and men, herbalists, healers, seers and midwives, were persecuted, tortured and executed by the religious and the secular authorities. They were accused of consorting with the devil, kissing his buttocks, causing hail and other human scourges. This genocide closed the way for modern humanity to get in touch with the invisible dimensions of existence, and opened the way to the absolute domination of reason.

A woman, hunched over and as old as the Earth, comes hobbling out of the house.

Early in the morning, while the children were still asleep, the old woman comes and grabs Hansel and puts him in a cage. Then she goes to Gretel, shakes her to wake her up and cries: "Get up, lazybones! Fetch some water and cook something good for your brother. He is locked in a cage and must be fattened up. And when he is fat enough, I will eat him!" Gretel began to weep bitterly, but it was all in vain. She had to do what the witch demanded.

What follows is a famous passage that is supposed to prove how foolish wise women, healers and seers are. The witch is supposed to ask Hansel to stick his finger through the bars to feel if he is fat enough. Instead of a finger, Hansel each time sticks out a little bone, presumably the remains of one of the witch's victims. The witch has poor eyesight and does not see the deception. Finally, after three weeks, she loses patience and starts preparing for the feast, even though Hansel is still "thin as a rake". In keeping with the requirement to burn witches, Gretel seizes the moment when the old woman looks into the stove to see if it's hot enough and shoves her into the fire to burn like so many other unfortunate women accused of witchcraft.

From here on, the story gets back on track, so we can reasonably assume that the episode with the cruel witch was inserted after the genocide of the wise women had begun. Hansel and Gretel set off on their journey home with the jewels of wisdom they received from the wise old woman in the magic little house.

After walking for three days, they arrive at a wide river. "We can't cross it," says Hansel, "I cannot see a walkway or a bridge." Then they see a white duck swimming across the water. They ask her if she would take them across. Just like the white bird that had shown them the way to the magic house, the duck now put them on its back and carried them to the other bank. Time and again, the seekers of truth and love are offered the help of the creatures of nature.

The Star Money

There was once upon a time, a little orphan girl whose father and mother had died. She had no home, not even a bed to sleep in. All she had left were the clothes on her back and a little piece of bread given to her by a kind-hearted man. Forsaken by all the world, she set out into the world.

Eventually, she reaches a field and meets an old beggar. He asks her: "Ah, give me something to eat, I am so hungry." The girl hands him her entire piece of bread.

Then a child comes along crying and says, "My head is so cold. Give me something to cover it with!" The girl takes off her cap and gives it to him.

After a while, she meets another child without a jacket. He complains about how cold he is. The orphan girl takes off her jacket and gives it to him.

Then she meets a girl without a dress. The orphan girl takes off her dress and gives it to her.

Then she comes into the forest and it is already dark. There she meets another child who asks her for a shirt. "It's already dark," thinks the orphan girl to herself, "no one will see me naked. I can give him my shirt."

But as she stands there with nothing on, stars begin to fall down from the sky, and when they hit the ground, the stars turn out to be silver coins. The next moment she feels a shirt made

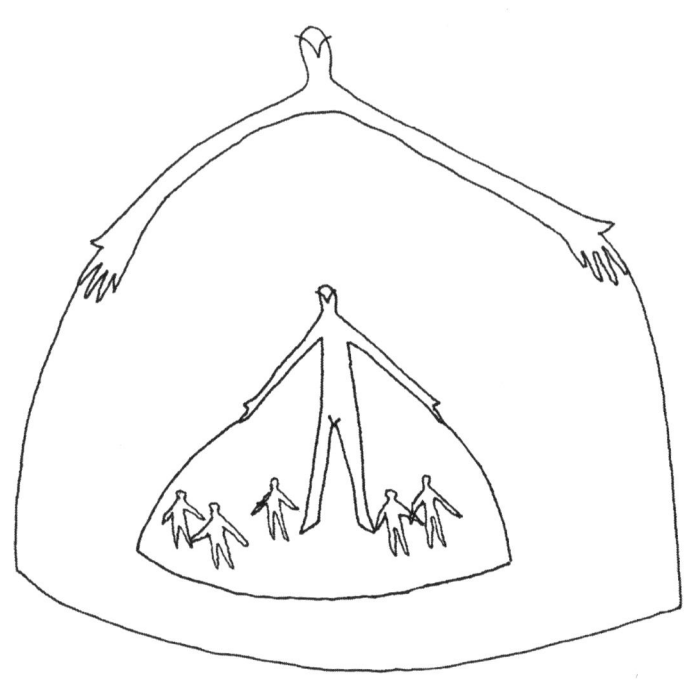

Good deeds are always rewarded.

of the very finest linen on her. She spreads it open and gathers the silver coins inside. She has been blessed with wealth for all her life.

This short tale accurately describes the revolutionary upheaval that awaits humanity in the spheres of economics and personal ethics. Instead of linear relationships based on the rule of give-and-take, on the exchange of goods or monetary exchange, we must tune in to the principles of a cyclical economy, best called the 'cosmic cycle of manifestation'. The orphan girl gave away all that she had and all that was asked of her until she was left naked. She expected nothing in return. The payment came back to her as a return flow of kindness and compassion in the form of a shower of silver coins. It is no coincidence that coins fall like stars from outer space.

I attribute a cosmic or universal value to the cycle of manifestation because it operates on a much wider scale than exchange. A person gives and does not expect to be paid for their gift. The gift is inscribed in the memory of the Universe. There, at the heart of the universe, it multiplies and endows the gift-giver with what they need – even if they are not rationally aware of their needs. The circle is not closed, as in an exchange, but open to surprises.

The purpose of being human is to create and to give to the world, to one's fellow human beings and to other beings. And the purpose of the Earth's existence as universal consciousness is to provide a return flow, to multiply the wisdom, power and love given, and to ensure that all who give selflessly receive all they need to live, create and enjoy.

The cosmic cycle of manifestation does not work unless it is supported by certain ethical values. The tale of the Star Money places selfless kindness, coupled with a sense of compassion, at the forefront. The second most important is the value of unwavering trust, which the orphan girl shows by being willing to be left naked in the middle of the night, even though her nakedness will be obvious to everyone when the day comes. But even before dawn, in the middle of the night, she is endowed with a shirt of the finest linen.

In third place, I place the value of modesty. By this I mean the renunciation of excessive desires or the will to possess. The cycle of universal manifestation works if a person does not expect more than they need. They may even need a castle, but only on condition that they actually need a castle in order to realise the meaning and purpose of their existence.

Rapunzel

Once upon a time there was a woman and a man who had long wished in vain for a child. Unexpectedly, they found reason to hope that their wish might come true. At the back of their house there was a small window overlooking the neighbour's magnificent garden which was full of the most beautiful flowers, herbs and vegetables. It was, however, surrounded by a high wall and no-one dared to enter because it belonged to an enchantress who had special powers. She was feared by all the world.

One day the woman was standing at this window, looking down into the strange garden, and she saw a bed planted with the most beautiful rampion (rapunzel). And it looked so fresh and green that she felt an irresistible desire to eat some of it. Because she knew that it was unattainable, the desire grew every day – she was completely consumed by it. She became paler and paler and more and more exhausted.

Her husband was frightened and asked her: "What ails you, dear wife?" "Oh," she replied, "if I do not have the rampion from the garden behind our house, I shall die." The husband, who loved his wife dearly, thought, "I must not let my wife die, I must get her some of the rampion, whatever the cost." At dusk, he climbs over the wall, quickly picks a handful of rampion, and brings it to his wife. She eats it eagerly.

It is important to note that the magic garden is at the back of the house, and we can only see it through a small window. Assuming this fairy tale is about certain mysteries of human being or existence, we can relate the symbolism of the little window to the mystery of what lies behind the human back. With our eyes we can only see the embodied world in front of us, so the space behind our backs is considered to be a symbol of the invisible dimensions of the Earth, the Universe, and also of humanity. We are referring to the causal world which contains the archetypes or matrixes that determine the way the everyday or embodied world is shaped and functions.

The magic garden is a perfect representation of this causal dimension of space. Beds with different types of vegetables, herbs and flowers can be imagined as individual archetypes or matrixes, in which certain values and forces are arranged and connected, which in the next phase have a decisive influence on the nature and orientation of the world in which we live.

The woman's craving at the sight of a bed of green rampion means that, as a representative of the human race, she has discovered in the causal dimension of the Earth an archetype or matrix of something that does not yet exist in the human world – something that the human being clearly wishes to experience or embody; hence the woman's inevitable desire to taste a handful of rampion.

Can the rampion, with its appearance in nature, and with its shape and colour, tell us anything about the discovered archetype? Rampion is one of the few varieties of lettuce that grows freely in the wild and is extremely tasty. When I was a little boy, once a week a scrawny old woman would come to our house to sell my mother a small bowl of rampion she had picked in the fields. Rampion is shaped like a rosette with leaves dancing around its centre. It resembles the chakras, the vital energy centres of the human body, known from the Indian yoga tradition.

Through a small window at the back of the house,
the woman fell in love with the delicious rampion.

With its lush green colour, it could symbolise the heart centre, which is usually represented by the colour green.

The rampion from the garden tasted so good to the woman that by the next day her desire for more had grown threefold. If the husband was to have any peace, he would have to climb into the garden once again. As it was getting dark, he climbed over the wall again, but as soon as he was on the other side, he was terribly frightened. The enchantress, the owner of the garden, appeared before him. "How dare you," she said with an angry look, "to climb into my garden and steal my rampion like a thief? You will pay for this."

The man begs for mercy, saying that he has only decided to steal out of extreme necessity. "My wife saw your rampion through our window, and would have died of desire if she hadn't eaten a little of it." The enchantress calms down and allows the husband to take as much of the rampion as he wants, on condition that he hands her the child when his wife gives birth. "It will do well and I will take care of it like a mother," the enchantress promises. The terrified husband agrees to the condition. Shortly afterwards, the wife gives birth to a baby girl. Immediately after the birth, the enchantress appears, takes the baby girl with her and names her Rapunzel.

First of all, we should free the enchantress (also known as witch in some versions of the tale) from the curse attached to the name. The word is derived from words like 'enchanting' or 'enchantment' (also in the sense of magic), which in themselves have no negative connotations. They not only denote human creativity, but also express an activity of other beings that goes beyond what can be logically perceived and explained.

In this sense, the enchantress of the magic garden can be seen as the guardian of the causal world and its archetypes and forces. Where human beings are allowed unhindered access to the causal worlds in their search for scientific knowledge, they can disfigure the physical world and its beings through irresponsible and unconscious actions. Unfortunately, these limits are already being transgressed and violated by the manipulation of human DNA, the misuse of nuclear power, the genetic manipulation of plants and the like.

In the enchantress I recognise Gaia, the creator and guardian of the Earth's Universe. She reveals herself as the teacher of humanity, who knows the way to the power of the heart and, as the story unfolds, leads humanity from one station to the next on the path to the knowledge of powers and qualities of the heart.

Rapunzel became the most beautiful child under the sun. When she was twelve years old, the enchantress locked her in a tower that stood in a forest and that had neither a door nor a stairway, but only a tiny little window at the very top. Rapunzel had magnificent long hair, as fine as spun gold. When the enchantress wanted to enter the tower, she stood below and called out: "Rapunzel, Rapunzel, let down your hair." When Rapunzel heard the enchantress's voice, she untied her braids, wound them around a window hook at the top and let her hair fall down twenty cubits, and the enchantress climbed up it.

As already indicated, the tale of Rapunzel acquaints us with the various aspects of the human relationship to the power of love and its all-encompassing values. In the first, most simple phase of the relationship, we are dealing with the concept of desire. The human being feels the existence of a power and value so overwhelming and attractive that he cannot refuse it. He does not understand or even think about what it is, but instinctively follows his feeling beyond the bounds of what is rational and logically perceptible, in order to be able to experience the unknown value of love.

Now, at the lonely tower, we reach the second stage in humanity's journey to the mystery of his own heart system. At this stage, the wife is replaced by her daughter. The latter learns the secrets of the heart not from her mother – that is, within the sphere of the human family – but from the enchantress, Gaia. A lonely tower in the middle of the forest represents a stop on the way to the heart, where the Earth itself appears as a teacher. Therefore, we cannot yet speak of a revelation of one's own heart-love dimensions. The school of the heart is now at the elemental level. It takes place in the natural environment and along the golden braid. I associate Rapunzel's braid with the human spine and the flows of life forces along it. Each time the enchantress climbs the golden braid to the window of the heart, it is a symbolic message that the elemental love from the treasury of the Earth's heart rises up via our spine to our human hearts, and from there inspires our love for the whole world of existence.

Unfortunately, the modern human being has almost completely forgotten the Rapunzel within him. Therefore, the power of human love is not strong enough to overcome selfishness and self-centredness, both in secular and spiritual respects. Love flows within the narrow circle of one's own family or religious or ethnic community. Fellow human beings or beings of other species who do not fit these criteria do not receive love, but rather its opposite in the form of hostility or even hatred.

The primordial force of love does exist in us, but in a dormant state.

A few years later, the king's son is riding through the forest and sees an unfamiliar tower. From a single window, he hears a song so beautiful that he stops to listen. It is Rapunzel, who was passing the time by singing with her sweet voice. The prince wants to climb the tower, but he can't find any doors. He rides back home, but the song has touched his heart so deeply that he returns to the tower every day to listen to it.

One day, as he is listening behind a tree, he sees the enchantress approach and call out, "Rapunzel, Rapunzel, let down your hair!" Rapunzel lets down her braids, and the enchantress climbs up them to the only window.

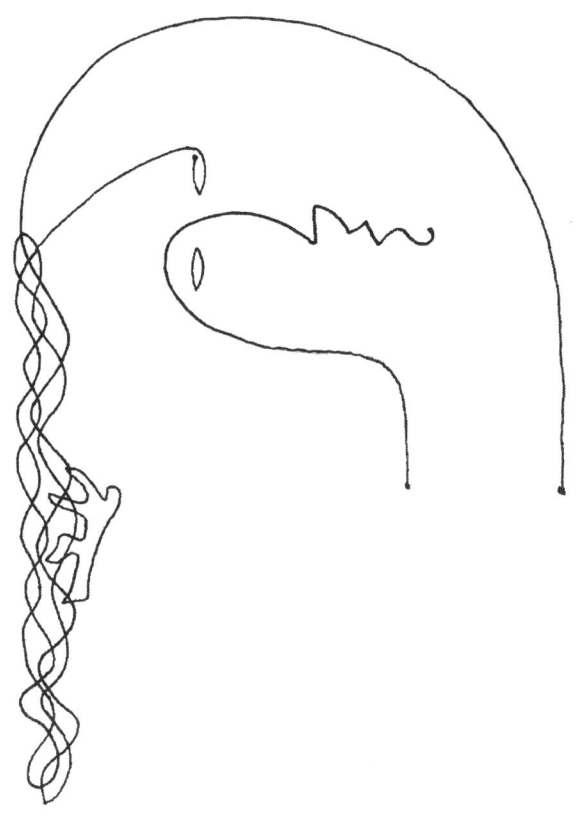

The prince climbs Rapunzel's
braid to get to her lonely home.

"If this is the ladder into the tower, then sometime I will try my luck," the prince thinks to himself. The next day, just as it is beginning to get dark, he approaches the tower and calls out, "Rapunzel, Rapunzel, let down your hair!" In an instant the hair fell down, and the prince climbed up.

At first, Rapunzel is terribly frightened, as she has never seen a man before. The prince begins to speak to her kindly, telling her that she has touched his heart with her singing. Rapunzel loses her fear, and when the prince asks her if she would like to be his wife, she agrees. They agree that the prince will come every night and each time bring a strand of silk for Rapunzel to weave a ladder and finally climb down onto solid ground.

As I have already pointed out in the case of Cinderella, the king, prince or queen in Grimm's fairy tales typically represent dimensions, usually called 'cosmic'. This does not mean that they necessarily originate from the Universe. I am referring to dimensions that transcend any human capacity to comprehend – they are all-encompassing. In the encounter between Rapunzel as Gaia's adopted daughter and the prince, we are dealing with an interaction and a connection between the elemental power of love and love as a cosmic force that flows through all creation from eternity to eternity.

At this point of the discovery of the values of the heart, the elemental power of love begins to connect in human beings with the angelic dimension of the heart, capable of sustaining the cosmic whole in harmonious motion and creation. Woman and man, as representatives of the two sources of love, are experienced as equal partners in the tale of Rapunzel and as such plan their descent to Earth together. What is missing is the embodiment of their already established relationship; the embodiment in everyday life. Hence the design of the strands of silk.

For now, their relationship is still secret, which means that it is manifested as an internal process. Rapunzel has indeed conceived a child (this is not mentioned in the fairy tale, of course), but how is she to give birth to her expected child in a tower without doors and without the conditions necessary for motherhood?

The enchantress did not notice anything suspicious until one day Rapunzel said to her, "How is it possible that you are more difficult to pull up than the prince, who simply jumps up and is already up here?" The enchantress realises she is being played – she is outraged and declares Rapunzel a godless child. She grabs her golden braids, wraps them twice around her right arm, grabs a pair of scissors with her left hand, and cuts them off. She takes Rapunzel to a lonely cottage in the middle of the forest, where she lives in misery and solitude.

The witch ties the cut-off hair to a window hook and waits until evening, when the prince comes and calls out: "Rapunzel, Rapunzel, let down your hair!" Then she drops the braids of hair to the ground, the prince climbs up and finds himself in front of the enchantress.

"You have come for your beloved," says the enchantress scornfully, "but that little bird is no longer in her nest, nor is she singing any more. The cat got her, and now she's going to scratch your eyes out as well, so you'll never see her again!" In his despair, the prince throws himself from the tower and falls into the thorns, which scratch his eyes out. For years, he wandered blindly through the forest, occasionally feeding on a strawberry or two, weeping and wailing for his beloved wife.

We are seemingly confronted with the wickedness of a ruthless enchantress. But in reality, we are faced with the painful process of transformation that a person, as a member of the human race, must undergo if he is to embody the value and power of love in his everyday life. This is not an easy task, because we are talking about the value of love in all its breadth and depth. Rapunzel and the prince develop such a value during their meetings in the lonely tower, elevated high above the ground of everyday life.

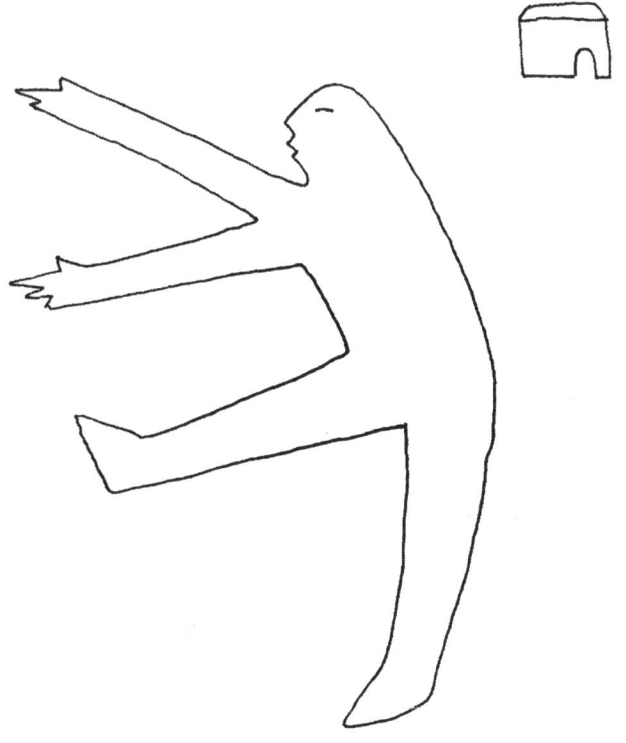

The prince wanders blindly
through the vast forest,
unable to find his home.

Both the feminine and the masculine aspects of the modern human being are facing a decisive test. A passage in the story resembles the Biblical Expulsion from Eden. Previously, the Earth, in the form of a magical woman, had provided people with everything they needed to survive and to sustain their community. Now, in isolation, the woman has to work hard to support her two children, the twins she has since given birth to.

The masculine aspect of the modern human being has found himself blinded by the rational view of life, which Grimm's fairy tales often speak of as the curse of our age. He has lost the memory of his true origins and the purpose of his existence in the firmament of the Earth.

One day, the prince wanders near the hermitage where Rapunzel lives with her twins, a girl and a boy. He hears the familiar sound of her singing, follows it and arrives at the door, where Rapunzel recognises him and throws herself into his arms, crying. Two of her tears fall into his eyes, and he can see again. He immediately takes the little family back to his kingdom, where they live happily and contentedly ever after.

The tale of Rapunzel seems to conclude with a 'happy ending', which in fact is not the case. There are two messages at the end that I would like to draw attention to. First, let's consider the voice of Rapunzel's singing, which helps the man wandering in the woods to find his way to his beloved wife and his warm home. Let us call it the voice of primordial love. We should listen to it in our hearts so that we can find the direction in our lives, at every moment, that will lead us towards the fulfilment of the purpose of our existence on Earth.

I would also like to draw attention to the two tears of Rapunzel. They fell on her husband's blind eyes and restored his sight. In this case, the healing and creative power of the element of Water is revealed when water is infused with the values of mercy, love and joy. Here, water is celebrated as the agent that enables love to become creative in everyday life – beyond what human reason deems possible.

The Devil With the Three Golden Hairs

There once lived a poor woman who gave birth to a baby boy. He was born in a magic caul. The latter is considered a sign of good luck, so it was prophesied that in his fourteenth year he would have the king's daughter for his wife. Soon after, the king, disguised as a peasant, comes to the village and asks the villagers what news they have. They tell him about the lucky new-born, saying that he is to marry the king's daughter when he turns fourteen. The king is wicked-hearted and asks the parents to let him have the child, saying that he will take good care of him. At first, they refuse, but when he offers them a sack of gold, they consent, believing that, being a child of good fortune, nothing bad can happen to him.

The king puts the baby in a basket, rides away to a wide river and throws the basket into the water, thinking, "I have freed my daughter from her undesired suitor." However, the basket does not sink but floats downstream for two miles and comes to a halt on the mill-dam. The miller's apprentice spots it and pulls it ashore, thinking he has found a great treasure. When he sees that he has rescued a baby, he takes it to the miller. As the miller and his wife had no children, they happily adopt him and raise him to be a fine and strong boy.

It happened that once during a storm, the king sought shelter in the mill. He sees the strapping boy and asks the miller and his wife if he was their son. "No," they reply, "he was washed up on the mill-dam as a baby fourteen years ago." The king realises that he is looking at the child of good fortune which he had thrown into the river. He asks if the boy could take the letter to the queen, and offers them two gold pieces as a reward. "As you wish," say the foster parents in unison. The letter read: "As soon as the boy arrives with this letter, let him be killed and buried, and all must be done before I come home."

But the boy got lost on the way and wandered into a dark forest. It was already dark when he spotted a small light in the distance. He hurries there and finds an old woman sitting by the fireplace quite alone. She tells him that he has wandered into a house of thieves. Although she warns him about them, the young man is not afraid. Tired to death, he lies down on a bench and falls asleep. The robbers come home and read the letter. They take pity on the boy and tear up the letter. Their leader, who surprisingly knows how to write, writes another message, saying that when the boy brings the letter, he should marry the king's daughter immediately. When he reaches the palace, they do as the letter says, and because the young man is good-looking and upright, the king's daughter does not resist.

After some time, the king returns to his castle and is surprised to find that the prophecy has come true. He asks how it could have happened, and finally says angrily to the groom: "A king's daughter is not so easy to get as a wife. If you want to keep her, you must bring me three golden hairs from the head of the devil." The young man is not afraid of the devil and immediately sets off.

The opening part of the tale tells us that human life in the embodied world unfolds along two threads. So far, we have seen that guiding thread which directs the path of life along the plan which the human soul – or the soul-human – draws up while still in the afterlife, in preparation for a particular incarnation. It imprints it in its mental memory and tries to carry it as intact as possible through the gates of birth. The story presents it in the form of a caul (magic skin) in which the boy was covered at birth.

The plan, drawn up with the help of spiritual masters and ancestors, has an inner power of its own. There may be forces at work in the world that are not in favour of the fulfilment of humanity's plan – like the malevolent king in the case of our tale – but we must keep believing. Life and its forces find a way to bypass the obstacles in the way and eventually realise the divine plan of the given embodiment, which we carry written in the deep layers of our memory.

The last paragraph of the tale, however, makes it clear that the plan for the given embodiment does not unfold of its own accord. It also requires personal engagement. In order to develop our own independent creativity, life presents us with challenges that we could not have known about when we were making the plan for our embodiment in the silence of the spiritual world. The miller's boy has indeed married the king's daughter, as prophesied, but the king does not recognise her as his wife without undergoing a dangerous test and the unknown difficulties that come with it. He has to pull out three golden hairs from the devil himself.

On his way to hell, the hopeful bridegroom passes by a town where the watchman by the gates asks him what his trade is and what he knows. "I know everything," replies the young man. "Then tell us why our market fountain, which once flowed with wine, has now become dry and no longer gives even water." "I will tell you when I come back from hell," he replies.

Then he passes by another town, and there also the gatekeeper asks him what his trade is and what he knows. "I know everything," the young man replies. "Then tell us why a tree in our town which once bore golden apples now does not even put forth leaves?" "I will tell you when I come back from hell," the young man replies.

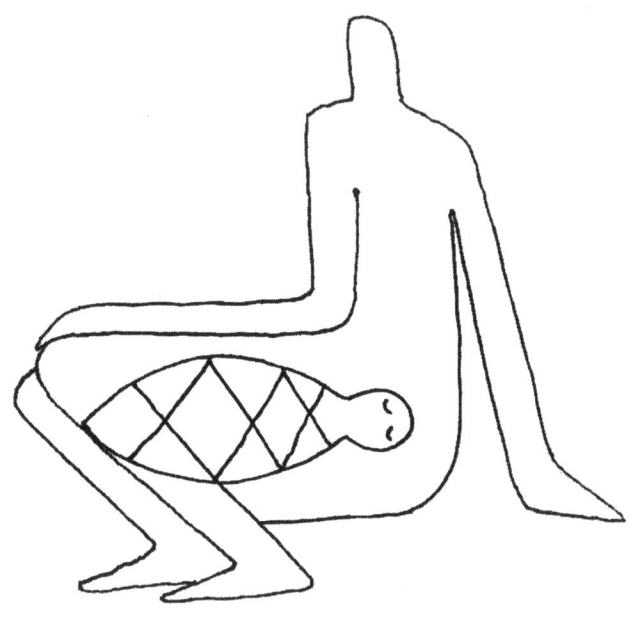

A person is born within the
totality of their being.

Then the child of fortune arrives at a wide river and calls for a ferryman. The ferryman asks him what his trade is and what he knows. "I know everything," replies the young man. "Then tell me why I must always be rowing backwards and forwards, and am never set free?" "I will tell you when I come back from hell," the young man replies.

All three tasks that the young man receives on his journey are related to the unfortunate circumstances in which the human being of the Iron Age found himself. According to historical sources, this begins a millennium or so Before Christ. Yet deep in the subconscious of the human race lies the memory of a golden age when peace and natural prosperity reigned on Earth under the sign of the culture of the Goddess.

Once upon a time, water carried with it ten times more life force than it does today. This is the meaning of the transition from water to wine in the language of fairy tales. Back then, in what the ancient Greeks called the 'Golden Age', apples had as much nutritional power as if they were gold. Today, however, apple trees are basically struggling to survive and might not bear any fruit at all if it were not for human care and fertilisation.

Isn't it true that one of the problems of the Iron Age is the perpetual serfdom of the ferryman? Where is the freedom of creativity if one is forced to constantly worry about mere survival?

The young man facing his ordeal finally arrives at the entrance to hell. It is dark inside, and the walls are covered with soot. The devil is not at home, but he finds his mother sitting in a large armchair. She does not look so evil when she asks him, "What do you want?" The boy explains to her the problems with his marriage and the related task of bringing the three golden hairs from the devil's head to the castle. "That is a good deal to ask for," she says, "when the devil comes home and finds you, it will cost you your life, but as I pity you, I will see if I can help you." She turns him into an ant and hides him in the folds of her dress. The young man does not forget the three tasks he was given on the way here, explains them in detail, and asks the devil's mother to find out the answers from the devil. "Those are difficult questions," says the devil's mother, "but just be silent and quiet and pay attention to what the devil says as I pull out the three golden hairs one by one."

In the evening, the devil returns home, eats his supper, then puts his head in his mother's lap to clean him of his lice , then falls asleep.

The scene with the devil's mother and her son is surprising – as if it were not set in hell. The mother shows mercy and offers her selfless help to the prospective bridegroom. The mother puts the devil's head in her lap and asks her to clean him of his lice. Given the circumstances, we can assume that we are not dealing with the devil and his mother at all. Can we trust the feeling that our protagonist has met Sister Earth and her partner?

In ancient Greek tradition, Sister Earth is called Gaia and her partner Pan. Since the tale had to go through the Middle Ages, when the Christian Church tried to suppress humanity's primordial love for the mother of life and for her masculine aspect (which uses his flute to keep the power of nature flowing), they had to be moved to hell. Only there are they allowed to continue to exist.

For centuries, the ideology of Christianity has sought to detach people from the Earth and to tie them to a God who exists beyond immediate life. Indigenous cultures found it difficult to come to terms with such an abstract notion of the divinity and, on top of that, with God as an autocrat. The experiment would have been doomed to failure had Christianity not at the same time proclaimed a curse on the Gaia-Pan pair. It even used the classical image of Pan with goat's horns and hooves to illustrate the figure of the devil as God's adversary and the seducer of the human race.

Isn't it striking that the devil in our story has golden hair – even though there may be only three of them? It is not that he

The young man, hidden in the folds
of the devil's mother's skirt, listens
to the answers of her son, the devil.

possesses gold, but his hair is gold as part of his being. That alone suggests that we are dealing with some cunning deception.

When the devil falls asleep, his mother pulls out his first golden hair. He is awakened by the pain and cries out, "What are you doing?" "I had a bad dream, so I grabbed your hair." "What did you dream about?" "I dreamt that a fountain in a market place from which wine once flowed has dried up, and not even water would flow out of it – what is the cause of this?" Surprisingly, the devil knows the cause: "If only people knew ... There is a toad sitting under a stone in the well. As long as it is there, the wine will not flow," says the devil, and falls asleep again.

The answer to the second question and the second hair pulled is similar. The devil reveals the secret of the withered tree, which used to bear golden apples, but now does not even turn green. In this case, the cause is a mouse that is eating away at its roots. He also threatens his mother with a slap if she wakes him up again with her dreams.

Of course, the mother was not dreaming, but had tricked the devil into giving her the answers to the young man's questions. The latter, transformed into an ant, listens attentively. When the mother pulls out the third golden hair, the devil jumps to his feet and is furious with the mother, but she calms him down, saying that she is not to blame for her bad dream. "What were you dreaming about now?" asks the devil curiously. His mother tells him a story about a ferryman who could not find anyone to take his place. This time the devil advises that when the first passenger comes and wants to go across, he must put the pole (which he uses to push the raft away) in his hand and jump ashore, and he will be free from his eternal duty. When the devil goes about his business in the morning, the mother gives the young man his human shape again, gives him the three golden hairs from the devil's head and sends him on his way home.

The devil's answers to the three unfortunate circumstances tell us that the devil is not some evil being, but a deity of the

Earth who has taken the form of the devil. How else would it know the secret of the dried-up well and the withered tree? The cause of the misfortune is not visible to the human eye. In both cases, obstructing forces are at work beneath the Earth, in its causal dimensions. Only someone at home in the deeper dimensions of the Earth's Universe can see the hidden causes of ecological disasters.

As we have said, Christian ideology has appropriated Pan, the ancient God of Nature, and transformed him into the devil. It has taken Pan's famous flute out of his hands and driven him from the fragrant plains of the Earth's landscapes into the dark and fiery underworld. The transformation of the joyful God of Nature into the cruel God of Hell is an ideological-political project to temporarily secure power and control over human beings as creatures of nature.

In my work with the Earth's landscapes, I have come to know Pan as the partner of Gaia. To the extent that Gaia is constantly giving birth to life from the womb in the interior of the Earth, Pan is responsible for the flow of life streams across the Earth's surface. His energy centres are spread across the landscapes of the embodied Earth. They serve all embodied beings, especially plants and animals, as reference points of contact with Gaia's creation. In the absence of original names for the two divine beings of the Earth's creation, we have borrowed both names from the ancient Greeks, who still had some knowledge of the feminine and masculine aspects of the Earth's totality.

Now we can understand how the devil, as a distortion of Pan, can know that there are forces and alien beings working underground on Earth who want to steal from Earth and its generations the knowledge that flows in the memory of water. I am referring to the knowledge of how to transform the currents of life into currents of wisdom and happiness – symbolised in our tale by the fountain that flows with wine instead of water. He knows because He has access to the Earth's memory.

On the other hand, he also knows that there are forces and alien beings working underground on Earth who are trying to steal from Earth the knowledge of how to transform matter into a spiritual substance capable of sustaining a heavenly quality of life on Earth – symbolised in our tale by the apple tree that bears golden apples. The first and second golden hairs from Pan's head represent the current tragic state of the Earth Kingdom. And the third golden hair is intended for us humans. It teaches us how to break out of the cycle of a superficial existence unworthy of a human being. But to understand the message of the third hair, we have to wait for the end of the story.

On his way home, the fortunate young man stops in both towns where he has been asked for help. He tells them what needs to be done to restore the heavenly quality of the Earth, for which he is handsomely rewarded. He returns to his bride with two donkeys laden with gold. Now the wicked king can no longer deny him his bride.

But the greedy king is tempted by the gold. He asks the bridegroom where he got it, hoping to find some for himself. The young man replies that it can be found on the other side of the river, where an old ferryman is taking travellers across. It lies there on the shore instead of sand. The greedy king hurries to the ferryman. He takes him to the other side of the river, pushes the pole into his hand and jumps onto the bank. As Pan (the devil) had predicted, the king could not get rid of the pole, and he has earned his daily bread by ferrying across the river ever since.

As promised, the meaning of the third hair from the devil's head is only revealed at the end of the story. Human beings must overcome their fears in the face of the embodied world. If they become greedy and accumulate wealth out of fear for survival, they will sooner or later lose their divine essence, degrading themselves from the status of a king to a servant of imaginary needs.

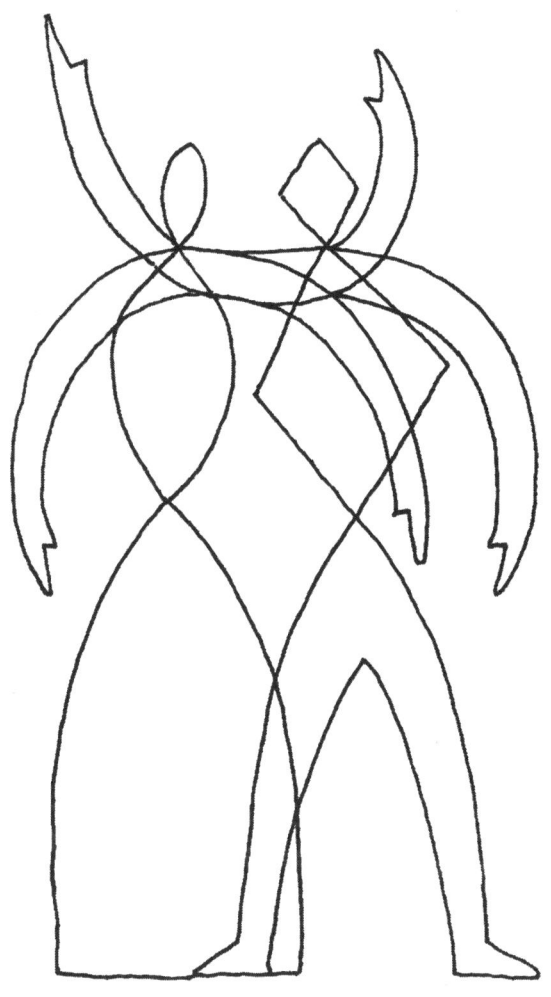

No one will ever be able to take the bride away from the fortunate young man again.

The Story of the Fisherman and His Wife

Once upon a time, there was a fisherman and his wife who lived together in a pot by the sea, and the fisherman went fishing every day; and he fished and fished. One day he sat by the rod and looked into the clear water; and he sat and sat.

Then the line went deep down to the bottom, and when he brought it up, he pulled out a large fish, that said to him, "Listen, fisherman, I beg you, let me live, I'm not a real fish, I'm a cursed prince. What good will it do to you to kill me? Put me back in the water and let me swim." "Well," said the man, "you needn't say so many words; I would have let go a fish that could talk anyway."

So he put it back into the clear water, and the fish went to the bottom, leaving a long trail of blood behind it.

If two people live in a pot and a fish can talk like a human being, then it cannot be otherwise than that we are not dealing with the dimension of the embodied world, but with a causal level that exists in the background of the manifest world, yet not too far away, because the fish is swimming in the water and the two characters in the story are behaving like normal people of embodied everyday life. To blur the discrepancy between the two levels, the narrator offers the mind an aid to understanding by mentioning that the talking fish is an enchanted prince. However, we can safely disregard this statement, as it lacks the usual request of enchanted princes in fairy tales to be freed from his fate.

But if the talking fish is not an enchanted person, what is it? It could be a mythical fish, described in the traditions of various peoples as the giant fish that carries the World Disc on its back. Its movements determine whether life on the manifest plane is harmonious or devastated by earthquakes or floods. In the tradition of my Slovenian homeland, the World Fish is called 'Faronika', derived from 'Pharaonika', because the tale of the giant fish was associated with the biblical story of the Exodus of the Israelites from Egypt, in the course of which the Egyptian soldiers drowned in the Red Sea while pursuing the Israelites. A folk ballad about 'Faronika' reads:

> *Jesus is swimming in the sea, in a deep sea.*
> *A fisherwoman swims after him, the fisherwoman Faronica.*
> *Ah, wait, fisherwoman, wait, fisherwoman Faronica!*
> *We want to ask you what's going on in the world!*
> *If I beat my tail,*
> *the world will end!*
> *If I turn on my back*
> *the world will be flooded!*

In a similar German folk song, the World Fish 'Concelebrant' is named after the first word of the Latin missal, because the first letter 'C' has the curly shape of a fish. A traditional text from the Eifel region goes thus:

> *The fish is the concelebrant.*
> *He is called the concelebrant in all the Masses of God.*
> *If he is not mentioned in all the masses of God,*
> *then there will be Earthquakes in the land.*

The World Fish with the
World Disc on its back.

It is clear that in both versions the World Fish is synonymous with the highest spiritual authority, in one case Jesus, in the other God. Translated into today's language, this would mean that the World Fish is a divine being associated with earthly phenomena such as earthquakes and floods. Consequently, we can equate the World Fish with Gaia, the creator of the Earth. The creative quality of Gaia is confirmed in the Grimm Brothers' tale of the fisherman and his wife by the fact that the talking fish, as we shall see later, is able to manifest all sorts of things on the surface of the Earth, from a cottage to a royal palace and more. Gaia here stands for the all-encompassing Earth consciousness that connects all the entities of the terrestrial universe and enables all the creative processes through which everything that exists can appear in embodied form.

In the fairy tale, the fisherman went back to his wife in the pot after his experience with the fish. "Tell me," said the wife, "didn't you catch anything today?" The fisherman told her about his encounter with the talking fish, and the wife said he should ask the fish for something in return. He could give them a cottage, she said, because she was not content to live in a pot forever. The man didn't have a good feeling about this, but he went back to the sea anyway, so as not to contradict his wife. But when he got to the water's edge, it was no longer as clear as it had been, but green and yellowish. So he stood there and shouted out:

> *Flounder, flounder in the sea,*
> *Come, I pray thee, here to me;*
> *For my wife, good Ilsebil,*
> *Wills not as I'd have her will.*

Then the fish came swimming up and asked: "Well, what does she want?"

"Oh," said the man, "my wife thinks I should have asked for something in return for letting you go. She doesn't want to live in a pot any more, she wants a cottage."

"Retrun to her," said the fish, "she already has one."

Upon this the man went back, and his wife was no longer sitting in a pot, but sitting on a bench in front of the door of a charming little cottage. Then his wife took him by the hand and said to him, "Come in, look, it's much better this way." So they went in, and inside the cottage there was a small entrance hall and a splendid living room and a chamber where there was a bed for each of them.

In the tale there are six encounters between the fisherman and the fish, triggered by the woman's desire for a certain manifestation – the described manifestation of a cottage is only the first of these. The encounters always take place in three stages. The first is the woman's desire for a certain object, followed by the man's magic spell, and in response the process of manifestation of the given object – in our case the cottage – is set in motion by the World Fish/Gaia.

The tale of the fisherman and his wife reveals in its detailed fairy tale language the secret of how the embodied world is realised. On the one hand, we have the human family and on the other the total consciousness of Gaia and her co-creators. Humanity has a feminine and a masculine aspect. While the feminine aspect of a given culture or civilisation focuses on the awareness of the daily life of the community, how it can live well and happily – symbolised in the fairy tale by a cosy cottage – the masculine aspect stands for the task of sending a message to the World Soul through appropriate invocations or rituals in order to bring about the corresponding manifestations. The magic spell *"Flounder, flounder in the sea, Come, I pray thee, here to me; ..."* opens communication with the World Fish/Gaia and sets the process of manifestation in motion. Of course, this only applies to a time when wishing did help, and it still had an effect in medieval European culture, where the collected fairy tales of the Brothers Grimm originated. But even indigenous peoples of our time, such as those of the Amazon, are still closely connected to the mystery of the natural world.

The enthusiasm for the cottage lasted no more than eight or fourteen days, when the woman said: "Listen, man, the cottage is too small, and the yard and the garden are so small, the fish could have given us a bigger house. I want to live in a big stone castle. Go to the fish and ask him to give us a castle."

The man was reluctant because he was happy with the nice cottage, but the woman persisted. In the end he had to go, even though his heart was heavy and he said to himself: "This is not right."

When he came to the sea, the water was all dark purple and blue, thick and grey, and not at all the green and yellow it had been the last time. Nevertheless, he stepped forward and said:

> *Flounder, flounder in the sea,*
> *Come, I pray thee, here to me;*
> *For my wife, good Ilsebil,*
> *Wills not as I'd have her will.*

"Well, what does she want?" asked the fish.

"Oh," said the man sadly, "she wants to live in a big stone castle."

"Go back to her, for she's at the door," answered the fish.

Upon this the man set out thinking he was going home, but when he got there, there was a big stone castle and his wife was standing at the top of the stairs. She took him by the hand and said, "Come in."

It is striking that the World Fish creates a stone palace without further objection, although it is obvious that the woman's desire for such a comfortable dwelling is not appropriate. However, the threatening backdrop set up by the description of the sea shows us that the woman's desires are not in harmony with the overall consciousness of the Earth. As the tale says: 'When the fisherman came to the sea, the water was all purple and dark blue, grey and thick'. The archetypal water in which the World Fish lives represents Gaia's emotional force field through which her wisdom and knowledge of the Earth's elemental consciousness is expressed. The described state of the water warns humans not to work against the laws of life. But how is it that the woman's arrogant idea of wanting to own a castle is nevertheless realised by Gaia?

The apparent contrast between the statement of the Earth's emotional force field and Gaia's willingness to create the castle can be understood in the light of the original contract between Gaia and humanity. We must imagine humanity as a vast multitude of souls to whom the Earth Creator once made the Earth available as a space for their unfoldment. From that time onwards, people have the possibility to embody themselves over again and over again on Earth, in order to gain experience and develop spiritually and ethically. They are allowed to have both constructive and destructive experiences, without Gaia and her teaching elemental spirits being allowed to intervene in a judgmental way.

Our story continues to unfold in the same manner. Gaia gave the fisherman and his wife not only a well-equipped castle, but also a large, luscious garden with the most beautiful flowers and fine fruit trees. Then the man said: "Now we will live in the beautiful castle and be happy." And they went to bed. But the next morning, when the woman saw the vast country stretching out in front of the castle, she nudged the man in the side with her elbow and said, "Get up and look out the window! Look, can't we be rulers of all this land? Go to the fish, and tell it our wish."

Since the man was not interested in being king, the woman said, "If you don't want to be king, then I will be king." The man did not agree and hesitated, but in the end, he went back to the

Fisherman's Wife on the Royal Throne

sea's edge. When he got there, he saw that the sea was completely black-grey and the water in it was fermenting, producing a foul stink. He stood there and recited the spell we know so well:

> *Flounder, flounder in the sea,*
> *Come, I pray thee, here to me;*
> *For my wife, good Ilsebil,*
> *Wills not as I'd have her will.*

Having become king, the woman soon wanted to become emperor, and as that was still not enough, she also wanted the papacy and ended up sitting there with three crowns on top of each other. At this point the woman had gone through the usual medieval hierarchy, from simple fisherman's wife to king, emperor and pope. Each time the man came to the sea with a new covetous desire, the sea had grown darker and was stirred up by gales.

Let us look at the folly of the woman in the mirror of our own time, so as not to be overwhelmed by the fairy-tale images. When we look at the world today, we see a civilisation that has almost completely conquered the Earth and shamelessly robs it of everything it needs for its hugely ambitious projects; whether that be building skyscrapers or tanks and sending rockets to the moon. None of this promotes the inner development of humankind, nor does it show any intention of both taking the above-mentioned contract between humanity and Gaia seriously and implementing it gradually. Why do we need bombs that can kill a million or more people at a stroke? And why does a simple fisherman's wife need papal prestige?

But this is not just about the ethical discrepancy between what humans want and what Gaia offers. The chaotic state of the sea, the increasingly dark and gloomy colours and the storms that pass over it indicate that something has gone fundamentally wrong in the background of the causal world in which the World Fish lives, something for which humanity is responsible. The elemental consciousness of the Earth is forced to bring into the world of form all sorts of things that do not serve life, or even poison or kill certain life processes. For all the objects and form-giving processes manifested by humanity, substances are extracted from the Earth, be it oil, ores to extract uranium and other metals, or water, which is the basis of all life processes. Modern humanity takes all of these gifts for granted; unlike indigenous cultures, which used rituals to thank the Earth for everything they took from it, modern humanity just demands more and more from Gaia, the World Fish.

In our story, the fisherman's wife sits like a log on her high papal throne, while all the kings and emperors kneel before her, kissing her shoes. The man thinks that now that she has risen to the highest papal rank, she can have no more desires – but far from it! When she wakes up one morning and sees the sun rising from her high bed, she is overcome by an irresistible desire to rule the sun and the moon and to become God.

"Go straight to the fish," she commanded her husband, "I want to become like God."

"Oh, wife," said the husband, falling on his knees before her, "the fish can't do that, he can only make you emperor and pope; I beg you, go inside yourself and stay pope."

At this, she burst into a rage, and her hair flew about her head so wildly that the fisherman saw no way out, and ran to sea as if out of his mind.

Is there not much in today's world that reminds us of the fisherman's wife's insane idea of becoming like the Almighty? Is the story of the fisherman and his wife prophetic in this sense? Just look at the rapid development of artificial intelligence, which even its inventors are now warning against, because they realise that they cannot control it; or the collective presumption that they are able to reverse the dangerous development of the transformation of the Earth. Huge projects are being funded to explore other planets or even to send spaceships to distant star systems, while our Earth, rich in natural resources, continues to be plundered and its previously fertile soil, with its diverse flora and fauna, is being transformed into a desert landscape. Behind this is the concrete will to usurp the creative abilities of Gaia and her divine helpers and to transform the planet Earth – and presumably the human body as well – in such a way that humans become independent of nature. This would also separate these humans from the elemental beings and forces of Gaia – which would be tantamount to a process of death.

When the fisherman reached the shore, the storm was so violent that the trees and houses were blown over, the mountains were shaking and the rocks were rolling into the sea. Even the sky had turned pitch black and there was thunder and lightning, as the sea rolled in black waves as high as church steeples and mountains, crested with white. The fisherman shouted, unable to hear his own words:

> *Flounder, flounder in the sea,*
> *Come, I pray thee, here to me;*
> *For my wife, good Ilsebil,*
> *Wills not as I'd have her will.*

"Well, what does she want?" asked the fish.

"Oh," said the man, "she wants to be like the good Lord."

"Return to her, for she's already back in the old pot."

Again, I want to emphasise that the words of the World Fish are not a punishment. They are a serious warning. To understand this, we need to imagine what it means to be 'in the old pot'. An embodied human being can hardly sit in a pot, but a soul can, because it knows no physical expansion.

'Being in the old pot' is a reference to the spiritual world of ancestors and descendants; the pot represents the spiritual realm in which human souls dwell before they embody themselves in the life processes of the Earth, and of course also after their Earthly death. In fact, the fisherman and his wife lived in a pot even before the World Fish Gaia gave them a cottage and thus an embodied living space. Prior to that they lived in the spiritual realms, and they inhabit them again, once their less than desirable experience on the manifest Earth plane ended in a most dramatic way.

The abrupt end of the fairy tale can ultimately be understood as a call to us humans to stop our arrogant demands on the World Fish/Gaia. Embodied life should once again be valued as a fantastic opportunity to gain physical experience and to bring happiness to our fellow human beings and the elemental world of nature. An immediate collective conversion of humanity is hardly to be expected. Therefore, it is up to us, as awakened individuals and groups, to take the first steps to ensure that we do not lose the right to incarnate time and again on Earth and to enjoy the gifts of embodied life in the name of humanity.

One-eye, Two-eyes and Three-eyes

There is much debate about how our star-studded realm came into being: This fairy tale is unique in that it gives us a glimpse into the creation of our terrestrial universe.

But we should remember that the Earth, with all its spatial dimensions and the beings and developments within it, is also a relatively independent universe. We can imagine that the history of its creation goes back to a distant epoch before the material Earth – as we know it today – even existed. The fairy tale of One-Eye, Two-Eyes and Three-Eyes tells – in an imaginary language – the story of the origin of the physical universe and its development up to the present day and perhaps even beyond.

Once upon a time, there was a woman who had three daughters, the eldest was called One-Eye because she had only one eye in the middle of her forehead, the middle one was called Two-Eyes because she had two eyes like all other human beings, and the youngest was called Three-Eyes because she had a third eye in the middle of her forehead in addition to her two eyes. Because Two-Eyes looked like other human children, her sisters didn't like her, and taunted her: "You with your two eyes are no better than ordinary people, you don't belong with us." They pushed her around, gave her only their discarded clothes to wear, their discarded food to eat, and caused her heartache wherever they could.

The very first words of the tale suggest that the story is about two different qualities of time and space. The fact that Two-Eyes, like other human beings, is endowed with two organic eyes confirms that she belongs to planet Earth, the planet on which humans and other beings such as plants, animals and minerals are endowed with a material body. Whereas the two sisters are endowed with either one or three eyes, which distinguishes them from the earthly sphere. We might equate them with a realm of cosmic development that unfolds on a plane where the existential form of embodiment does not occur. In our fairy tale this unknown realm is associated with the concept of the 'third eye'. In Hinduism and other world views, the 'third eye' is often drawn on the forehead as a symbol for the pineal gland, which is located in the centre of the brain and is regarded as the gateway to spiritual life.

In our context, we can understand this to mean that the two sisters with a third eye on their foreheads belong to a development that is not connected to the Earth, but rather to an extraterrestrial development. The bad treatment of Two-Eyes by her two 'extraterrestrial sisters' can be explained by the fact that she – as part of the earthly evolution – is perceived as alien.

When the Earth or Gaia, as a conscious being, began to develop within its own evolutionary peculiarity, it violated the known cosmic order. This new development, which encompassed more than the creation of our biological bodies and associated eyes, was not welcomed by the original rigid cosmic world order. As a result, it was disrupted and weakened in a number of ways, as we will find out later on in the fairy tale.

It happened that Two-Eyes had to go out into the field to look after the goat, but she was still very hungry because her sisters had given her so little to eat. So she sat down on a little hill and began to cry, and she cried so much that two little streams ran down her cheeks. And when she looked up at one point in her lamentation, a woman stood beside her and asked,

The three sisters

"Two-Eyes, why are you crying?" Two-Eyes replied: "Shouldn't I cry? Because I have two eyes like other people, my sisters and my mother don't like me, they push me from one corner to another, throw their old clothes at me and give me nothing to eat but their leftovers."

The wise woman replied gently, "Two-Eyes, dry your face, I want to tell you something that will ensure you no longer go hungry. From now on, just say to your goat:

> *Bleat, my little goat, bleat,*
> *Cover the table with something to eat.*

and a table will be set before you with the most beautiful food, and you can eat as much as you want. And when you are full and no longer need the table, just say:

> *Bleat, my little goat, I pray,*
> *Take the table right away,*

and it will disappear before your eyes."

Everything happened as the wise woman had said, and Two-Eyes ate her fill and was very happy and content.

The story of the birth of the Earth's universe has begun!

Let us first examine the role of the goat in our tale. It symbolises the wonderful abundance of life on our Earth and feeds the hungry two-eyed creature. Why the goat? The goat is considered one of the most intelligent animals. I knew a mathematics professor from Macedonia who kept goats to feed his family during the last world war. When he was struggling with a difficult mathematical problem, he would go out to be with the goats. Whenever he found the right solution, all the goats would stand up at the same time.

The goat represents the elemental power and intelligence of nature. Pan, the ancient Greek god of nature, has the body of a goat. And who could be the wise woman who makes Two-Eyes aware of the ubiquitous yet overlooked gifts of the earthly universe? We might associate her with Gaia, the creator of the Earth. She shows Two-Eyes that the general lack of abundance of life on Earth from which human beings suffer is only a superficial phenomenon. If we, as individuals or as a civilisation, were to connect with the underlying (elemental) intelligence and power of Earth and Nature, there would be no hunger or lack.

It is obvious that the redemptive relationship with the elemental forces of nature comes about through a magical formula. If we decipher the language of the fairy tale, we discover that the desired reconnection cannot be achieved through a specific technology or the use of artificial intelligence, but through a conscious exchange. The little magic table is summoned when it is needed and then returned. It is the cyclical exchange with the elemental consciousness of nature that can work wonders.

When Two-Eyes' sisters notice that she is no longer interested in the scraps they throw at her as food, they become suspicious and begin to search for the reason, even insisting on accompanying Two-Eyes to the pasture to find out her secret. At first, One-Eye tries to observe what is happening, but she falls asleep and when she closed her eye, Two-Eyes was able to summon the table with all its treasures and enjoy the meal. Later on, Three-Eyes accompanied her sister to the meadow, where she also fell asleep and closed two of her eyes, but was able to keep her third eye open and watch the amazing exchange between the goat and her sister. When she told her mother, the latter took a butcher's knife and plunged it into the goat's heart, causing it to drop dead.

How does this dramatic turn of events come about? Many clairvoyant people speak of a highly developed civilisation on Earth called Atlantis, which lived in harmony and peace with the subtle levels of Earth and Nature, like Two-Eyes with the goat and the little table. But Atlantis was brought down by the influence of a dark power from the deep universe, which initiated a warlike phase on Earth, causing dramatic upheavals in the earthly universe. As a result, the wonderful subtle form of the Earth was lost and it solidified into the form we still experience as matter today.

Where does this 'dark force' come from that motivates the mother of One-Eye and Three-Eyes take a knife and stab the goat in the heart? It is possible to imagine that there are two different currents in the evolution of the vast galactic space: one, denoted by the third eye in one-eyed and three-eyed beings, that is centred – symbolically speaking – in the head. It is strictly hierarchical and power-hungry. Any kind of heart-based relationship is alien to it and we can equate it with the concept of coldness. It is not difficult to see its influence and outcomes throughout the world.

The second current in the evolution of our relatively young universe is associated with the concept of warmth. It grows organically from the dimensions associated with the heart and strives for revelation in the embodied world. The fate of Two-Eyes is symbolic of this second current, carried by the impulses of love. It appears to be weaker because, in an earthly context, it is supported by only a few awakened individuals and groups. However, it has an enormous inner power due to its interconnectedness with beings from different levels and dimensions – I am thinking of ancestral souls, elemental beings, angelic and faery worlds, etc.

Now we can listen to the rest of the tale with confidence.

When Two-Eyes saw that her goat had been killed, she went out into the field, sat down on a hill and wept bitterly. Suddenly the wise woman stood beside her again and said: "Two-Eyes, why are you crying?"

"Should I not cry?" she replied, "The goat that set my table so beautifully every day when I recited your little saying was stabbed to death by my mother; now I must suffer hunger and sorrow once again."

Then wise woman advised her: "Ask your sisters to give you the entrails of the slaughtered goat and bury them in the ground outside your door, and it will be your good fortune."

Since the sisters considered the entrails worthless, they agreed to her request. Two-Eyes took the entrails and buried them quietly outside the front door at night.

When they awoke the next morning and went out the front door, there stood a magnificent tree with leaves of silver and fruit of gold, yet none of them knew how the tree had appeared during the night. Only Two-Eyes knew that it was the exact spot where she had buried the goat's entrails.

The entrails of the slaughtered goat give us the key to answer the question: remember that the structures of the intestines and the brain are very similar. Colloquially, for example, we speak of a gut feeling when we make a decision based on emotion. Since we have identified the goat as the embodiment of the elemental intelligence of nature, we can say that the goat's entrails reveal a deeper level of existence. If the goat represents the elemental consciousness of the Earth and nature, then its entrails would represent a deeper world, which in the language of fairy tales is called the world of dragons. This is the deepest level of the earthly realm, home to the cosmic creative power and wisdom that is able to re-manifest the life of the Earth in its beauty and perfection at any moment. The silver tree with its golden fruit, which grew from the entrails of the goat and thus from the archetypal world of the dragons, is a symbol of this.

In summary, we can say that the first part of the tale, with the goat and the richly laid table, represents the first phase of the earthly genesis of the world. In this phase we could imagine the Earth as a paradisiacal space, characterised by a happy exchange between human beings and the wise Sister Earth and her living world. This ideal world collapsed with the catastrophe

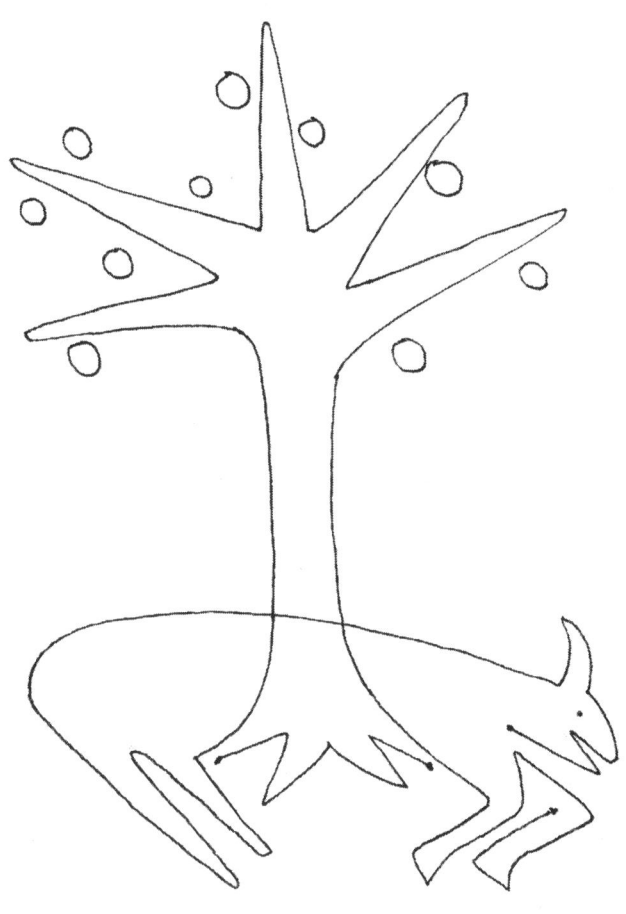

Tree of Life grown from
the entrails of the goat

of Atlantis – in our case with the stabbing into the goat's heart. In the second phase of world creation, which we are currently experiencing, the Earth Cosmos is being re-founded on a deeper level of existence. We equate this with the primordial wisdom of the dragons. A new, forward-looking kind of reality is emerging, emanating from the archetypal heart of Gaia, symbolised by the silver tree with the golden fruit.

When the mother saw the beautiful tree, she said to One-Eye: "Climb up, my child, and break the fruit from the tree." One-Eye climbed up, but when she tried to grab one of the golden apples, the branch snapped out of her hands, and this happened repeatedly, stopping her from being able to pick a single apple, and it was the same with Three-Eyes.

Then Two-Eyes said: "I'll try it too, maybe I'll succeed."

And indeed, the golden apples did not retreat from her, but fell into her hands, so that she could pick them one by one, and bring down a whole apronful. The mother took the apples, and as One-Eye and Three-Eyes were jealous of Two-Eyes, who alone could pick the fruit, they treated her worse than ever before.

This sequence shows us that the silver tree with the golden fruit is not a romantic phenomenon from the past. On the contrary! Its very presence speaks directly to our present situation, clearly expressing that in the future it will no longer be possible to enjoy the gifts of life from Gaia and Nature without at the same time lovingly connecting with the essence of the Earth. The fruit of the Tree of Life could not be harvested by One-Eye and Three-Eyes because they treated their sister unkindly.

Unfortunately, I have to say that this version of the Grimm Brothers' tale lacks a logical conclusion. Instead, like so many times before, we have the arrival of a prince at the end, who is enchanted by the beauty of Two-Eyes, and takes her to his castle as his future bride. Fortunately, I am sometimes given the opportunity to look into the network of universal memory – a kind of cosmic Internet. In the version I see there, the three